"*Who Is My Neighbor?* is a theology text, a leadership manual, a Bible study, a missions tutorial, and a path to finding personal purpose. From the Word to the world, Steve Moore challenges your mind and stirs your heart for your neighbor."

—LEITH ANDERSON, president, National Association of Evangelicals, Washington, DC; pastor, Wooddale Church, Eden Prairie, Minnesota

"Steve Moore challenges us to take a new look at a familiar biblical principle in the context of our fast-paced, ever-changing, and closely connected world. With passion and wit, he reminds us how our actions today can impact the world of tomorrow as our 'neighborhood' expands."

—SAMMY T. MAH, president/CEO, World Relief

"Our vertical relationship with God is measured by how we horizontally connect with those around us. This is the message at the heart of *Who Is My Neighbor?* Steve Moore injects within the narrative of our twenty-first-century reality the primacy of vertical connectivity resulting in prophetic witness that reconciles the energy of social networking with a kingdom culture imperative stemming from the Good Samaritan parable. Definitely a must-read."

—REVEREND SAMUEL RODRIGUEZ, president, National Hispanic Christian Leadership Conference

"The question posed in the title of this book is one that has been bandied around for centuries. However, the depth to which Steve Moore probes this question is fresh, compelling, and convicting. It is a call to action for the twenty-first century. This book is a must-read for every person who is a Christ follower. Your interior world and your exterior world will be forever transformed."

—JO ANNE LYON, general superintendent, The Wesleyan Church; founder/chair, World Hope International

"Most of us suffer from compassion overload. The media wears us out with their daily dose of suffering and injustice. In this intriguing book, Steve Moore goes against conventional wisdom by explaining how 'the curses of globalization can become blessings of increased opportunity to serve others.' I highly recommend this book as a back-to-the-basics look at rethinking the lesson of the Good Samaritan in our global village."

—HANS FINZEL, president and CEO, WorldVenture; author of *The Top Ten Mistakes Leaders Make*

"In a globalized world where your neighbor can be anyone, anywhere, it's hard to know how to be the Good Samaritan. A few hours with this book will reveal a simple path to discovering what God is inviting you to do with your life."

—MICHELE RICKETT, founder and president,
Sisters In Service; coauthor of *Forgotten Girls*

"I loved this book. It is engaging, fresh, deep, simple, complex, profound, and well written. Quite simply, it reflects the heart of Jesus. I found myself underlining, writing notes, and thinking of how I could get this into the hands of our leadership. This book deserves a wide audience."

—BUDDY HOFFMAN, senior pastor, Grace Fellowship Church,
Snellville, Georgia

"We human beings have long been willing to complicate simple questions such as, 'Who is my neighbor?' And in today's hyper-connected, twenty-four-hour-news-cycle, smartphone world, we have high-definition streams of complicating possibilities piped into our living rooms. Using the time-honored wisdom of Jesus, Steve Moore helps us sort through sensory overload and compassion fatigue in a quest to discover our own core passions and find real neighbors to love."

—JIM MARTIN, vice president, church mobilization,
International Justice Mission

"I hope this book helps you as much as it has helped me think through and act to answer the question 'Who is my neighbor?' Steve Moore helps us deal with the shame and guilt we feel in not meeting all the needs of the planet in the twenty-first century. He carefully leads us through the process of making the right decisions by placing us in the position to deal with the poor, oppressed, and lost of our day according to the leading of God in our lives."

—AVERY T. WILLIS, executive director, International Orality Network

"What a great book! Steve Moore has given us a fresh look at the Good Samaritan. The reader will be challenged to rethink ministry compassion and to reflect the heart of God in our dealings with our neighbors. After reading this book, my heart burned with new passion to reach our world for Christ with the message of hope and salvation."

—DR. STAN TOLER, general superintendent, The Church of
the Nazarene Global Ministry Center

Being a Good Samaritan in a Connected World

# WHO IS MY NEIGHBOR?

Foreword by George Verwer

# STEVE MOORE

NAVPRESS

Discipleship Inside Out™

Discipleship Inside Out™

NavPress is the publishing ministry of The Navigators, an international Christian organization and leader in personal spiritual development. NavPress is committed to helping people grow spiritually and enjoy lives of meaning and hope through personal and group resources that are biblically rooted, culturally relevant, and highly practical.

**For a free catalog go to www.NavPress.com**
**or call 1.800.366.7788 in the United States or 1.800.839.4769 in Canada.**

ISBN-13: 978-1-61291-151-9

Cover design by Arvid Wallen

**Library of Congress Cataloging-in-Publication Data**
Moore, Steve, 1960-
  Who is my neighbor? : being a good Samaritan in a connected world / Steve Moore.
    p. cm.
  Includes bibliographical references.
  ISBN 978-1-61521-723-6
  1. Church work. 2.  Good Samaritan (Parable) 3.
Globalization--Religious aspects--Christianity.  I. Title.
  BV4400.M66 2010
  226.8--dc22

                    2010029399

Printed in the United States of America

1 2 3 4 5 6 7 8 9 / 15 14 13 12 11

OTHER BOOKS BY STEVE MOORE

*The Dream Cycle*
*While You Were Micro-Sleeping*

To Jean Charest, my first world Christian mentor. Thanks for opening my eyes to the nations and encouraging the initial baby steps of obedience for my first short-term mission trip that ruined my life for ordinary Christianity.

# CONTENTS

# FOREWORD

We have all heard the expression "You can't teach an old dog new tricks." I am glad that I am not a dog but a person created in the image of God and saved and set free by the reality and grace of Jesus, whom I trusted and believed in March 3, 1955, in a Billy Graham meeting in New York City. Even as an older person, by the grace and power of Jesus I keep learning and changing.

The heart passage of this amazing, passion-filled book, the story of the Good Samaritan, was one of the parables of Jesus that changed my life. So Steve's book quickly caught my attention, resonated with my own journey and passion, and now I want to see that many other Jesus followers read it and learn, and change.

After leading the ministry of Operation Mobilisation for forty-six years, from the very first trip to Mexico, I felt led to hand over the leadership to younger leaders. At that same time the call to cross the road in Jesus' name, spoken about in these pages, came into my life like a tornado out of heaven. It actually started when I visited a garbage dump in Mexico at nineteen, but did not really make its full impact until about eight years ago when I finally became fully convinced that proclamation of the gospel in all its many forms leading to disciple making and church planting must come together with social action and social concern.

This same understanding came to our entire movement, which now has over five thousand workers across more than a hundred nations. You can be sure many of them will want to read this book, as it's so much in the very vein that God has drawn us over this past decade. I only wish we had it ten years ago . . . or better yet fifty-some years ago when I first arrived in Spain with my wonderful young bride.

I never preached on the story of the Good Samaritan until this change started to take place in my thinking and theology. Now it is my number one passage. I have preached from this text in dozens of countries over a hundred times. Sometimes I even give an invitation at the end of my message for people to stand up in humility before God and pray, "Lord, make me a Good Samaritan." I feel many who read this book are going to cry out to God in a similar way. Many words and ideas will jump from its pages into your mind and heart: passion, the heart of God, the need for grace, others-focused—and yes—the beautiful name of JESUS.

Steve Moore has walked the walk. He has been a pacesetter for many and a servant at the same time. As I sat at his feet reading this book, I was helped, challenged, and inspired, becoming convinced that I should write these words and get involved with what God is saying in these pages. For me this means also buying hundreds of copies and getting them into the hands of potential readers, who in time have the potential to be the next generation of William Wilberforces, C. T. Studds, and Amy Carmichaels. Perhaps they will do still greater things than these.

The decision to cross the road for Jesus is yours. I challenge you to wrestle with the truths in this book, then "go and do likewise."

—George Verwer, June 2010
World Missions Advocate Founder,
Operation Mobilisation

# AUTHOR'S NOTE

In order to leverage changes associated with life in a connected world, this book is available in several formats, including the digital "freemium" version that may have introduced you to the physical product you hold in your hands. If you aren't familiar with the freemium version, visit www .whoismyneighborbook.com to learn how to give your friends free access to this content.

The digital version of this book includes links to videos supplementing the content of each chapter. You have access to this additional content at www.whoismyneighborbook.com. Every chapter includes a video prequel, a two-minute (or less) backstory on the big ideas being developed. In some chapters we included links to news stories or other ideas that have a video parallel on YouTube or other public sites. In other chapters we have invited organizations engaged in activities referenced in the book to contribute video footage that brings the ideas to life. We are giving you the "picture" and "the thousand words." The digital content is flagged with a simple icon 🎥, and it will signal you to go to www.whoismyneighborbook.com, where you will find links to web, video, and audio files that expand on the text.

Finally, in order to help you apply what you are learning and explore some ideas in more detail, we have included more than $100 of bonus content that you will discover as you read. In addition to an online assessment (MyPassionProfile.com, see page 81), you will have access to downloadable webinars from The Mission Exchange. Each bonus content item is available for free with a one-time-use discount code, and you'll find a brief description of the resources in the sidebars throughout the book. Discount codes for the bonus content are not available in the free-mium version of the book.

# ACKNOWLEDGMENTS

Working on this book has reinforced an African way of understanding life that says *I am* because *we are*. I'm indebted to the visionary board of The Mission Exchange, who quickly embraced this project and provided me with the flexibility necessary to meet extraordinarily short deadlines.

My colleague David Mays makes everything I write better with his candid and thoughtful feedback. My assistant, Mary Kay Palguta, embraced this project as if it were her own and with an indefatigable spirit pressed through to the finish line. I could not have pulled this off without her help. My wife, Sherry, served as a helpful reader and invaluable cheerleader. I am deeply grateful to Joe Trimmer, who invested many hours in recording, editing, and uploading video footage for this product.

Mike Miller and the NavPress team took a leap of faith to embrace the unusual approach to this project. Brian Thomasson's editorial input sharpened my thinking in subtle but significant ways.

Finally, I owe a continuing debt of gratitude to my parents, who modeled so effectively the message of this book and serve as my primary prayer partners. Thanks for your unwavering support and consistent intercession.

# INTRODUCTION

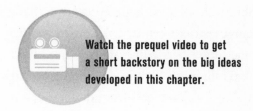

Watch the prequel video to get a short backstory on the big ideas developed in this chapter.

Who is my neighbor?

These four words served as the catalyst for a story, told by Jesus and recorded in the gospel of Luke, referred to as the Good Samaritan. In asking, "Who is my neighbor?" a religious expert was really asking Jesus, "When does God expect me to take responsibility for the needs of others?"

Jesus, as He often did, answered the man's question with a question of His own, prefaced by a story. At its core the parable Jesus told is about two very religious Jewish men ignoring someone who had been robbed, beaten, and left for dead along the side of the road. A third man, the Good Samaritan, went out of his way to provide practical assistance for the wounded traveler.

After telling the story, Jesus looked at the religious expert and asked, "Which of these three do you think was a neighbor to the man who fell into the hands of robbers?" (Luke 10:36). The obvious answer to Jesus' question is the Good Samaritan, which sets up the punch line for the entire conversation: "Go and do likewise" (Luke 10:37).

When Jesus told this story, it really wasn't possible to be a neighbor to others, on the order of the Good Samaritan, unless you were physically near them. If you weren't near them, you wouldn't even know about their needs, at least not soon enough to do anything meaningful to help.

Times have changed. We live in a wireless wonderland, an ocean of information with tweets, status updates, text message news alerts, customized home pages, and 24/7 news cycles that wash over our lives in endless waves. The accelerating impact of globalization driven by broadband Internet, Wi-Fi hot spots, web-enabled mobile phones, and search engines such as Google has powerful ramifications on the way we intuitively calibrate our responsibility for the needs of others. The adoption of mobile technology is happening faster than that of color TV in the middle of the twentieth century. According to *Fast Company* magazine, mobile phone subscribers will reach the five billion mark in 2010 with as many as two billion of them in developing countries. Mobile broadband is projected to surpass access from desktop computers by 2015.[1]

Now that you have access to the needs of the whole world in the palm of your hand by way of a netbook, iPad, or mobile phone, who really is your neighbor? How exactly has living in a Google-powered world complicated the answer to such a simple question? How do we assign a meaningful page rank to the virtual tsunami of human needs that flood into our lives from every corner of the world? How do we keep from being swept away in the tidal wave of shame and guilt that results from paralyzing inaction? How do I know when God expects me to be a neighbor to the wounded and hurting people on the side of the road in this global village?

When answering questions such as these, it is helpful to examine Good Samaritan opportunities in our day. We need to zoom in to personalize the needs of others and zoom out to get perspective on the big picture. First I want to introduce you to Eutisha Rennix, an African American from Brooklyn, whose story is a painful reminder of how proximity impacts responsibility.

One could easily imagine the thoughts racing through the mind of twenty-five-year-old Eutisha as she got ready for work on December 9, 2009. . . .

*Just sixteen days until Christmas and ninety days before my due date. How will I get everything done?*

She was employed at the Au Bon Pain coffee shop in Brooklyn. But the day would soon unfold with much bigger challenges than Christmas shopping or the final preparations for a new baby.

The first symptoms were shortness of breath, followed by intense pain in her abdomen. Since she was six months pregnant, it's easy to understand why her condition generated both urgency and uncertainty. Before long the pain became severe enough to warrant emergency action.

As luck would have it, the coffee shop in which Eutisha worked was about six hundred feet from the Fire Department of New York (FDNY) headquarters. The proximity of the FDNY headquarters provided the coffee shop with a regular base of customers. It was often filled with FDNY employees in their government-issued blue sweaters, along with EMS personnel and their top brass.

Shortly after 9:00 a.m., as Eutisha's symptoms escalated, colleagues raced to the front of the store looking for help. They discovered that two trained EMTs, with six years' and four years' experience respectively, were standing at the counter in uniform buying bagels. Eutisha's co-worker frantically explained that her pregnant friend was in need of medical attention. The two EMTs said they were on break and coldly suggested someone call 911. They did. Coincidentally, the Emergency Medical Services (EMS) dispatch center that handles 911 calls is located in the same building as Au Bon Pain, several floors above where Eutisha collapsed. Shouts from other employees warned that Eutisha was turning blue, but the EMTs appeared unfazed and left the coffee shop, bagels in hand.

By now an Au Bon Pain manager was involved, again asking for help from anyone in the store. Eutisha, still collapsed on the floor, had begun foaming at the nose and mouth. Two other "good Samaritans," as described by the *New York Post*, both FDNY employees, ran to the back office in an effort to provide assistance. By now several 911 calls had been placed, and paramedics arrived at 9:28 a.m., nearly thirty minutes after her initial symptoms. Eutisha, already in cardiac arrest, was transported to Long Island College Hospital, where she was pronounced dead at 10:17 a.m. Her six-month-old unborn daughter was too premature to survive, outliving her mother by just over two hours. She was posthumously named Jahniya Renne Woodson.

When information began to surface about the tragedy of Eutisha's death, Mayor Michael Bloomberg was among the first to speak out, using words such as "unconscionable" and "outrage." The story struck a chord with the national media, and people around the country responded similarly with disgust and unbelief. How could a twenty-five-year-old pregnant woman die with almost no emergency care, just six hundred feet from the FDNY headquarters, in the back office of a coffee shop bustling with EMTs, a few floors below the very 911 dispatchers handling the emergency calls?

The visceral push back to the tragic and bizarre circumstances of Eutisha's death is amplified by our intuitive understanding of how to gauge the level of responsibility we assign to individuals who are provided the opportunity to be "Good Samaritans," taking action in response to the needs of others. One's level of responsibility is determined, though none of us would consciously try to calculate it in these terms, by *proximity*, how close we are to what happened; *urgency*, how serious the need; and *capacity*, how qualified or capable we are to offer assistance or add value.

proximity + urgency + capacity = responsibility

The two EMTs at the counter who declined to get involved were a matter of feet from Eutisha (proximity). In fact, the entire FDNY was only six hundred feet away. The situation escalated to emergency status quickly (urgency) with a seizure that left her unconscious, foaming at the nose and mouth. A combined decade of experience as EMTs (capacity) suggested they were far better prepared than ordinary citizens to provide assistance, in spite of the fact that they did not have their equipment with them.[2]

This combination of proximity, urgency, and capacity translates into extremely high levels of responsibility, but what happens when the needs of others are not only tragic but also chronic and epidemic? By *tragic* I mean urgent, life-threatening, or life-altering; by *chronic* I mean ongoing problems or challenges that are unlikely to be solved quickly or easily. *Epidemic* refers to the scale or scope of need, affecting many people. How do we assign responsibility for action when the problems others face are every bit as tragic as Eutisha's but not limited to the critical minutes associated with first responders and on a scale that exponentially multiplies the need beyond one person to thousands or millions of people?

When the need is tragic, chronic, and epidemic, urgency is sustained, proximity becomes less relevant, and responsibility for action is much more difficult to assign. That's what makes Bant Singh's story so complicated.

In 2000, Baljeet Kaur, the teenage daughter of Bant Singh, a Dalit farmer in Punjab, India, was lured by a woman into the waiting arms of two men who raped her. Sadly, nothing about this incident is unusual. Dalits, literally "broken people," are on the lowest rung of the Hindu caste system and are viewed as untouchables, outcasts. Three Dalit women are raped every day; few are reported, and even fewer of the perpetrators are ever convicted.

Bant Singh was determined to defy the odds and pressed charges against his daughter's rapists, including the woman who lured her to them. In an interview with *Frontline*, Bant Singh said, "I was determined to get justice, but initially I was stopped by the village panchayat [village leaders]. They kept telling me not to go to the police. . . . They offered money. . . . They offered my daughter gold ornaments and a scooter. But I refused to put a price on my daughter's honor. We went to the police, and in 2004 the district court convicted three people—Mandheer Singh, a . . . man called Tarsem . . . and a woman, Gurmail Kaur, who had lured my daughter to these men."[3]

Justice for Bant Singh and his daughter came at a high price. The year after the conviction, he was assaulted twice by people connected to the rape. On both occasions the attacks were reported to the police but the alleged perpetrators were released on bail. On January 7, 2006, a group of assailants attacked again. This time they had a gun, but they only used it to coerce him not to run away. They beat him with iron bars and axes and, like the man in the story of the Good Samaritan, left him half dead.

Bant Singh's wife and family were notified of the beating and rushed him to a local hospital, where he was refused treatment because he was a Dalit. After lying untreated for thirty-six hours, he was transferred to another hospital, where both of his lower arms and one leg were amputated due to gangrene. Google his name and you will find videos of Bant Singh speaking from his hospital room, not only about his family's struggle but about the ongoing battle against oppression and exploitation facing millions of Dalits.

Bant Singh readily understands the personal tragedy of his daughter's rape, and the subsequent assault on his life is but one chapter in a bigger story. This is not only about a single Dalit farmer or that farmer's daughter; it is about a quarter of a billion Dalits in India and millions more throughout South Asia. The challenges they face are tragic, chronic, and epidemic.

Every seven days, three Dalits are murdered, five have their homes or belongings burned, six are kidnapped or abducted, and three Dalit women are raped. Baljeet Kaur, the daughter of Bant Singh, happened to be one of them.

When we learn about tragic circumstances such as Bant Singh's and the millions of Dalits in South Asia, we understand the urgency of chronic needs such as these will not be resolved in the time it would take for a 911 call to produce a first responder. The urgency of Dalit exploitation is similar and yet very different from that of Eutisha Rennix.

The same could be said about the needs of refugees in Darfur or the internally displaced people of the Democratic Republic of Congo, living in the dark shadow of violence due to conflict minerals, or the millions of children orphaned by HIV/AIDS in southern Africa.

When the need of others is tragic, chronic, and epidemic, urgency is sustained, proximity is made irrelevant, and responsibility for action is much more difficult to assign. While I realize you don't live in proximity to Dalit farmers or AIDS orphans and you probably don't know any Congolese women who have been raped or robbed or exploited, their needs—along with the needs of Darfur refugees or street children in Bucharest or adolescent girls trapped in South Asia's sex trade or literally dozens of other compelling examples of human need here and around the world—are no less urgent. And because the challenges these people face are chronic as well as epidemic in proportion, it is much more complicated to sort out how much responsibility we should accept in trying to make a difference, to be a neighbor.

The story of the Good Samaritan reinforces the basic understanding of how we ascribe responsibility to act on behalf of others: proximity + urgency + capacity = responsibility. At the time Jesus told this story, proximity was the primary variable affecting the level of responsibility one would have with regard to taking action on behalf of others. Without proximity it would be difficult if not impossible to even be aware of the need of another person in a time frame that would allow helpful action. Travel over long distances was difficult and time consuming, so even where the needs of others were both chronic and epidemic, little responsibility would be assigned to those who were not in close proximity to the people who were suffering.

Thomas Friedman, in his best-selling book *The World Is Flat*, explains how the combination of desktop computers and broadband Internet have flattened the world by giving more people access to more information more quickly than ever before. Faster communication and transportation continue to make the world flatter and smaller. Proximity is no longer the primary variable in ascribing the level of responsibility we have for others. I don't have to be near someone in order to know about her need, and even if I can't travel to where she lives, there are likely others with whom I could partner who have both the proximity and capacity to make a difference.

In our global village, answering this once straightforward question, "Who is my neighbor?" has never been more complicated. But I believe there are answers to this question that empower each of us to leverage our giftedness and resources in our areas of God-ordained passion and live in the sweet spot of a fulfilling and fully engaged life. This liberating lifestyle is free from the guilt of inaction and the messiah complex of over-commitment. It is not limited to missionaries or aid workers or professional spiritual first responders. It is for ordinary people like me and you.

The reality of a shrinking globe and the growing availability of smaller, faster technology do not make information overload inevitable. On the contrary, the curses of globalization can become blessings of increased opportunity to serve others. God is at work in this Google-ized world, and technological advances in the hands of Spirit-empowered Good Samaritans can set the stage for the "even greater things" Jesus said His followers would do (John 14:12).

I believe it is time to recalibrate our answer to the question, "Who is my neighbor?" To help you with this process, I've organized this book in three parts. In part 1 we'll take a fresh look at the story of the Good Samaritan with a focus on the one big idea in this parable. It is important that we understand what Jesus had to say in response to the question, "Who is my neighbor?" and what His answer meant to the people who first heard Him tell the story. That foundation will enable us to make more informed application for our lives today.

Part 2 of the book will explore the implications of living in a connected world on our responsibility for serving others. Google is one of the most visible brands associated with a connected world. It serves as a one-word metaphor for the impact of globalization, the flattening and shrinking of our world, and how we process and prioritize our biblical responsibility to be a neighbor to others. I believe Google's patented PageRank actually serves as a model that helps us prioritize our actions and focus our service on God-ordained passions. God uses life-shaping, Good Samaritan–like experiences to awaken and inform the passions within us, leading the way forward into opportunities to make a difference in the lives of others.

Part 3 explores the question, "What would Jesus describe as His highest priority passions?" I suggest that God, though engaged and concerned about everyone and everything, has expressed a special affinity for the ultrapoor, the oppressed, and those trapped behind a thick veil of spiritual darkness with little access to the gospel. While each of us can expect to have unique passions that inform our service of others, there is a sense in which each of us will reflect the heart of God in response to these universal priorities of the kingdom.

To get started on this journey together, I want to take you back in time, to the scene of the crime, for a closer examination of the words of Jesus about the traveler left for dead on the side of the road and the Good Samaritan who came to his assistance.

# Part 1

# RECONNECTING WITH THE GOOD SAMARITAN

Chapter 1

# REDISCOVERING THE GOOD SAMARITAN

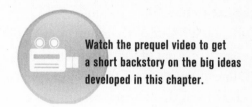

Watch the prequel video to get a short backstory on the big ideas developed in this chapter.

One of the reasons Jesus was such a master teacher is that He was a master storyteller. The parables of Jesus are rich with imagery and packed with meaning. The Good Samaritan has only 162 words and can be read at a comfortable pace in sixty seconds. But the lessons of this story echo through the centuries, like the timeless voices of a choir in a majestic cathedral, exhorting generation after generation to pursue an others-focused lifestyle that reflects the true nature of God.

The parable of the Good Samaritan is easy to read, but it is difficult to live, even for people who claim to follow Jesus, which is why my eyes were drawn to a news story with the title "Jerusalem Monks Trade Blows in Unholy Row."[1]

The traditional site of the crucifixion of Jesus is marked by the Church of the Holy Sepulchre. Six Christian sects stake a claim to this holy site on the rooftop of the church like squatters after a land rush. The delicate balance of power is managed by a "status quo" law established in 1757 by the Ottoman Empire. Yet under the surface the tension remains like the fault line of a tectonic plate that could unleash the hidden fury of a fanatical earthquake at any moment.

Ethiopians and Egyptian Copts have had an especially heated territorial dispute on the roof of the church for more than a century. The Ethiopians refer to the shrine as the House of Sultan Solomon, believing it was given to the queen of Sheba by the son of David, Israel's ancient king. They ceded control to the Egyptian Copts in the nineteenth century when they were unable to maintain a physical presence due to an epidemic. In 1970 the Copts were temporarily absent from the rooftop chapel, which opened a window of opportunity quickly seized by the Ethiopians, who have kept a monk huddled in the corner day and night ever since to stake their claim.

On a hot Monday afternoon in July 2002, an Egyptian monk moved his chair to get out of the sun and mistakenly (or not) crossed an invisible fault line into what the Ethiopian monk perceived to be his holy territory. To quote from the Reuters story:

> "They (the Ethiopians) teased him," said Father Afrayim, an Egyptian Coptic monk at the next door Coptic monastery. "They poked him and brought some women who came behind him and pinched him," he said. Each side accuses the other of throwing the first blow in the fist-fight and stone throwing that ensued. Police eventually broke up the brawl but by all accounts many of the protagonists were already wounded.

According to reports at least seven Ethiopian clerics and four Egyptians were injured in the fracas, including one broken arm. One monk was left unconscious and hospitalized. The anger continued to simmer the following day, like a volcano oozing lava, spewing the hot ash of angry words into the sky. An Egyptian monk hollered catcalls while simultaneously moving a hand across his throat, pantomiming the execution of his rival on the rooftop. He was surrounded by pieces of broken chairs and rocks like battlefield debris.

When I first read this news story, I didn't know whether to laugh or cry. You can't make this stuff up. The irony is palpable. It appears that claiming to follow Jesus and being close to where He actually told the story of the Good Samaritan do not make it any easier to do the neighborly thing. No wonder the key to the Church of the Holy Sepulchre has been passed down for centuries from father to son by a Muslim family, the only way to keep a modicum of peace at the site where the Prince of Peace is believed to have died. Clearly what the Samaritan did was good but not easy.

## STUDYING THE PARABLE

Putting the teachings of Jesus into practice does not come naturally for any of us. It requires careful thought and conscious effort. But before application comes understanding that builds on a commitment to ascertain the one overarching principle or idea that Jesus intended to communicate. A common danger is overanalyzing or allegorizing every detail of the story until you can't see the proverbial forest for the trees. The process of capturing the meaning of the *single thought* embedded in a parable involves a careful and prayerful analysis of the *setting*, *story*, and *sequel*.[2]

To understand the setting we have to look at the immediate context that triggered the story. Who was Jesus talking with, and what was the nature of the encounter? Why did He tell this story? To understand the story we have to remember that Jesus intentionally focused on common experiences, plucked like low-hanging fruit from everyday life. He wanted to ensure the characters and setting would be relevant to His audience. He captured the attention of His hearers by talking about people and places to which they could easily relate; His words were like a pool of still water in which they could see a reflection of their own lives.

The earthy, down-home approach to storytelling used by Jesus can work against our understanding of a parable. The culture and way of life in first-century Palestine were understandably quite different from what we experience today. When analyzing the story we need to be careful not to project meaning based on our worldview and culture that would not have been in the minds of the people to whom these words were first spoken. An important question to ask is, "What elements of this story will be difficult to understand without some level of historical and cultural background?"

Finally, in addition to the setting and the story, we must also analyze the sequel. In this case *sequel* refers to a result, consequence, or inference, not a second parable building on the first like a Hollywood movie series. In the sequel, Jesus often summarized the message or made specific application to primary members of the audience as identified in the setting.

Having looked carefully at the setting, story, and sequel, the primary focus of study with a parable is capturing the single thought it was intended to communicate in words that transcend the circumstances of the story. Once the single thought is clearly stated, there may be one or more supporting ideas that relate to the overarching primary principle.

With this simple framework in mind, let's revisit the story of the Good Samaritan, as found in Luke 10:25-37. I've omitted the verse numbers to help you immerse yourself in the narrative and inserted the study template to help you see how these components overlay on the parable. If you are like me and have benefited from hearing this story many times over the years, you will be tempted to skim over it quickly, perhaps not reading it at all.

When it comes to Bible study, familiarity is both a friend and a foe. It is our friend in that only after we have a basic feel for the facts will we be able to dig deeper into the meaning and application. It is our foe in that familiarity can be like a well-schooled pickpocket, deftly removing valuables from the wallet of our hearts without even rousing suspicion. Guard your heart; read slowly, carefully.

## THE GOOD SAMARITAN

SETTING: On one occasion an expert in the law stood up to test Jesus. "Teacher," he asked, "what must I do to inherit eternal life?"

"What is written in the Law?" he replied. "How do you read it?"

He answered: "'Love the Lord your God with all your heart and with all your soul and with all your strength and with all your mind'; and, 'Love your neighbor as yourself.'"

"You have answered correctly," Jesus replied. "Do this and you will live."

But he wanted to justify himself, so he asked Jesus, "And who is my neighbor?"

STORY: In reply Jesus said: "A man was going down from Jerusalem to Jericho, when he fell into the hands of robbers. They stripped him of his clothes, beat him and went away, leaving him half dead. A priest happened to be going down the same road, and when he saw the man, he passed by on the other side. So too, a Levite, when he came to the place and saw him, passed by on the other side. But a Samaritan, as he traveled, came where the man was; and when he saw him, he took pity on him. He went to him and bandaged his wounds, pouring on oil and wine. Then he put the man on his own donkey, took him to an inn and took care of him. The next day he took out two silver coins and gave them to the innkeeper. 'Look after him,' he said, 'and when I return, I will reimburse you for any extra expense you may have.'

SEQUEL: "Which of these three do you think was a neighbor to the man who fell into the hands of robbers?"

The expert in the law replied, "The one who had mercy on him."

Jesus told him, "Go and do likewise."

## THE SETTING

Jesus was anything but a politician, and yet He experienced the functional equivalent of "gotcha journalism" more than the average person running for office today. But Jesus' detractors were not merely trying to embarrass or discredit Him in order to undermine the support of His followers. They wanted to justify their belief that He was worthy of death. Wherever Jesus went, He had a contingent of detractors obsessed with the goal of producing evidence that would enable them to charge Him with blasphemy and put Him to death. Just a few chapters prior to the Good Samaritan, Luke tells us, "The Pharisees and the teachers of the law were looking for a reason to accuse Jesus, so they watched him closely" (Luke 6:7).

If this drama were being played out today, we could easily imagine the Pharisees and experts in the law spending hours in front of a whiteboard conducting brainstorming sessions about how and when they would launch their next plot to trip up Jesus. I can hear their fist-pounding arguments and feel the tension and frustration in the room rise. I imagine someone nervously pacing back and forth, responding to the latest idea with terse, cutting words: "No, He's too smart for that!"

Perhaps the expert in the Law who stood up to test Jesus in the exchange that led to the story of the Good Samaritan was among those Luke referred to a few chapters earlier, looking for a reason to accuse Jesus. Whether he was on an official mission or operating as a lone ranger, the question he posed, "What must I do to inherit eternal life?" was designed to put Jesus to the test (see Luke 10:25). But Jesus, like a skilled intellectual counterpuncher, turned the spotlight of the entire conversation back on the religious expert with a question of His own: "What is written in the Law? How do you read it?"

Without missing a beat, the public verbal sparring match with Jesus continued as the religious expert quoted from two passages in the Torah—first Deuteronomy 6:5, "Love the LORD your God with all your heart and with all your soul and with all your strength," then Leviticus 19:18, "Love your neighbor as yourself."

"You have answered correctly," Jesus replied. "Do this and you will live" (Luke 10:28).

The religious expert began trying to test Jesus. But now "he wanted to justify himself" (Luke 10:29). So he continued the exchange with a follow-up question of his own, "And who is my neighbor?"

Here's how Micah, an Orthodox Jew quoted by Ted Dekker and Carl Medearis in their book *Tea with Hezbollah*, describes this exchange: "In Judaism, that is a burdened question [Who is my neighbor?]. In the Mishnah, which is the summary of all interpretation of Jewish law, 'neighbor' is a technical term for friend. It basically defines neighbor as a practicing Jew, which is how the Pharisees in Jesus' time interpreted it."[3] Micah goes on to suggest the religious expert actually was trying to bait Jesus into redefining the meaning of *neighbor* in a way that would have  been scandalous to a sensible Jew. But Jesus outmaneuvered His antagonist again by telling a story instead of answering the question.

## THE STORY

When looking at the story it is important to identify any hindrances to our understanding, including historical or cultural differences that would color our perspective. Even if you have visited Israel, you probably don't have the ability to conduct a mental virtual tour of the location for this story and could benefit from a few simple background details to establish the context.

Jerusalem is higher in elevation than Jericho. Over a seventeen-mile stretch, the elevation drops three thousand feet; hence the victim was "going down from Jerusalem to Jericho." This was the most public road in all of Judea, the grand thoroughfare between these two cities. As many as twelve thousand priests resided in Jericho and would have traveled regularly on this road. Since the priest and Levite were also "going down," we can assume they were traveling from Jerusalem to Jericho. This is an important detail that the original hearers of this story would not miss. The priest and Levite were not reporting to the temple for service but rather heading back home, having served their duty.

Why is this so important? Jews who came in contact with a dead body were considered ceremonially unclean. Priests and Levites were especially diligent about avoiding impurities that could complicate their readiness to report for duty at the temple. Since these two were headed home, their ability to rationalize avoiding contact with a person left for dead along the road would have been undermined.

Author Ted Dekker describes the parable of the Good Samaritan, saying, "Like all good tales, his story had a strong antagonist, a killer who took a man, pummeled him within an inch of his life, and left him for dead. And it had a strong protagonist, a man who went out of his way to nurse the victim back to life after others refused to help the dying man."[4]

But perhaps more importantly, the parable had a dramatic and unexpected plot twist that would have stimulated repulsive angst in the minds of the original hearers. The hero of the story is not a Jew. This unexpected turn of events, positioning a Samaritan as the good guy, would have triggered an emotional gag reflex, as if the words of Jesus reached just far enough down the throat of the religious expert (and the others who shared his worldview) to make him want to spit them out. This part of the story is so important that we'll devote the entire next chapter to exploring it in more detail.

## THE SEQUEL

In the sequel to the story (remember, in this sense *sequel* is a result, consequence, or inference) Jesus once again turned the focus back on the religious expert. Having responded to the question with a story instead of an answer, Jesus now pressed the expert in the Law to answer his own question, "Which of these three do you think was a neighbor to the man who fell into the hands of robbers?" (Luke 10:36).

Without debating, arguing, or even so much as raising His voice, Jesus pinned His attacker in a trap of his own making. The question is so simple that even a child in the crowd could have answered it. It is so profound that it blew up the very worldview assumptions underlying the verbal exchange. The question that triggered the story was, "Who is my neighbor?" Jesus flipped the entire conversation on its head, changing the focus of the question by asking, "Which of these three was a neighbor to the man?" From Jesus' perspective the burden of responsibility is not on others to somehow qualify to become our neighbor. The responsibility is on us to take the initiative in being a neighbor to others.

The expert's disdain for this man of mixed race ran so deep that he couldn't even bring himself to say the word *Samaritan*, replying, "The one who had mercy on him" (Luke 10:37). His words were like the strands of a makeshift fuse, slowly burning, with the bomb of truth exploding in his own face as Jesus responded, "Go and do likewise" (Luke 10:37).

## THE SINGLE THOUGHT

As we touched on earlier, the goal of all this analyzing of the setting, story, and sequel is distilling a single thought, an overarching big idea that summarizes the main point of the parable in words that transcend the story itself. In some cases, Jesus specifically explained the meaning of a parable. Where He didn't, as is the case with the Good Samaritan, we are left with the challenge of carefully and prayerfully capturing the meaning, the single thought. It is impossible to remove all subjectivity from this process, and there is room for honest disagreement.

I distill the single thought from the Good Samaritan in the following sentence: *God expects us to take the initiative, crossing boundaries and overcoming barriers, to show His mercy by serving others.*

## SUPPORTING IDEAS

Once the essence of the parable is captured in a single thought, we can go back to the combination of the setting, story, and sequel to expose any supporting ideas that resonate with the overarching principle. Sometimes the supporting ideas flow from reliable comparisons we can make from items in the story that clearly were intended to be symbolic. In other cases the supporting ideas emerge as we put the puzzle pieces of the wider interaction together and get a glimpse at the cover of the box.

In the case of the Good Samaritan, there are no obvious comparisons or symbols. But when the story is viewed in context with the setting and sequel, several supporting ideas are worthy of consideration. First, *how you respond to the needs of others is determined by who you love the most.* Remember, the need for the story, why Jesus told it, is grounded in the religious expert's quoting of two important passages from the Old Testament that emphasize the priority of loving God and loving others.

The second supporting idea in this passage is *if you love God first, you will live others-focused.* Without telling us anything about the motives or beliefs of the Samaritan, Jesus paints a vivid, colorful picture of what it looks like in real life to love God most, to put God first. You take the initiative, crossing boundaries and overcoming barriers, to show His mercy by serving others. The challenge we face in applying this message to our daily lives is that our world is shrinking and the neighborhood is changing. We'll come back to that central issue, but first it is important that we understand how radically Jesus redefined the neighborhood of first-century Judaism by inserting the plot twist that made the hero of the story a Samaritan.

Chapter 2

# REDEFINING THE NEIGHBORHOOD

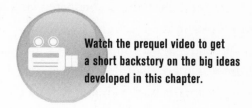

Watch the prequel video to get a short backstory on the big ideas developed in this chapter.

Jesus never used the descriptive words "good Samaritan." Search for this phrase in the New Testament with your Bible software program, and you won't get any results, unless your search feature includes chapter headings that were not in the original text. "Good Samaritan" is an extrabiblical label, a title that has been assigned to this parable, aptly reducing the essence of the story to two words.

For the average Jew listening to Jesus tell this story, the words "good Samaritan" would have been an oxymoron, such as "orthodox heretic" or "good bad guy." Samaritans were among the people Jews loved to hate. They were not viewed as neighbors, in part because they were from "the hood," the other side of the tracks. But in His paradigm-busting fashion, Jesus was about to redefine the neighborhood.

If we could interview the expert in the Law who approached Jesus in Luke 10 about the bad blood between Jews and Samaritans, he might respond by saying, "It's a long story." By some accounts the roots of this dispute reached back more than one thousand years from the time of Jesus to the relocation of the tabernacle by Eli from Mount Gerizim to Shiloh, which was perceived by some as the creation of a false place of worship and illegitimate priesthood.[1] With this tension in the background, the divide was institutionalized during the civil war that split the country in two, Israel in the north and Judah in the south. Omri, the sixth king of Israel, "bought the hill of Samaria . . . and built a city on the hill, calling it Samaria, after Shemer, the name of the former owner of the hill" (1 Kings 16:24).

Around 722 BC, the northern kingdom of Israel was attacked by Sargon II, an Assyrian ruler and "the people of Israel were taken from their homeland into exile in Assyria" (2 Kings 17:23). One of Sargon's strategies for dominating a conquered land involved the resettling of foreign peoples to the region in an attempt to dilute their culture and history. When foreigners intermarried with locals, as some in Israel did, the culture was more than diluted; it mutated. The people brought to the towns of Samaria by the king of Assyria did not worship the Lord. Their interest in the God of Israel surfaced only after they were attacked by lions and perceived it to be an act of divine judgment. They pleaded with Sargon II for instruction on how to appease this powerful "local deity" and eventually settled into a pattern of syncretism, blending together the worship of Yahweh with "their own gods in accordance with the customs of the nations from which they had been brought" (2 Kings 17:33).

In the sunset years of the Babylonian exile, when Ezra and Nehemiah returned to Jerusalem, Samaritans were viewed as the enemies of Judah and not permitted to join in the reconstruction of the temple or the city (see Ezra 4:1-3; Nehemiah 4:7). By the time of Jesus, one of the most insulting accusations that could be leveled against a Jew was to be called a Samaritan. Jews went out of their way to avoid contact with Samaritans, who were the social equals of stray dogs. Though violence between Samaritans and Jews was more the exception than the rule, the level of hatred and prejudice rivaled the deepest racial fault lines one could imagine today.

## BIAS-INDUCED BLINDNESS

Every culture has blind spots that filter out aspects of reality. One of the most difficult blind spots to expose is prejudice, especially when it is religiously justified. This bias-induced blindness inspires a hateful boldness that prefers the judgment of fire and brimstone over mercy and neighborly compassion. Prejudice of this nature is like being kidnapped by hatred and hauled away with a black hood over your heart. The darkness is subtle but real; it is the eyes of the heart that can't see. That was true of Jonah with the Assyrians as well as the disciples with the Samaritans. And lest you get on your high horse of pride, test your first response to groups such as Hezbollah, Al Qaeda, or the Taliban. Vengeance is the Lord's, and justice in the face of violence is the responsibility of governments. Our role as individual Christ followers is loving forgiveness.

Jesus saw prejudice against Samaritans in the heart of the disciples and went out of His way to expose it. John set the stage, saying of Jesus, "Now he had to go through Samaria" (John 4:4). In the Samaritan community of Sychar, Jesus had an amazing encounter with a woman He met at the well outside of town. The combination of tenderness and truth-telling in this story is a powerful example of the personal ministry of Jesus. In this unlikely setting, Jesus chose to reveal Himself as the Messiah to a Samaritan woman who in the eyes of Jews was twice removed from the mercy of Yahweh, first by her mixed-race birth and second by her promiscuous behavior. She had been married five times and was living with a man when she encountered Jesus.

The living water Jesus poured into the soul of the woman at the well overflowed into the town of Sychar, like the Nile of ancient Egypt, fertilizing the soil of their hearts, preparing the way for an abundant harvest. But there is a second layer of truth in this story that is easily overshadowed by the fruitful results of Jesus' personal ministry. Could it be there were two reasons Jesus "had to go through Samaria," on His way back to Galilee? In this unusual setting Jesus created His own rabbinical classroom, staging a powerful teachable moment in which He exposed the bias-induced blindness of His first disciples that kept them from seeing the needs of others.

When Jesus exhorted His disciples, saying, "Open your eyes and look at the fields!" they were standing in a Samaritan village, surrounded by people they loved to hate (see verse 35). They would not have chosen to be there, but Jesus "had to go through Samaria," first to reveal Himself to a Samaritan woman and second to challenge His disciples to see what God sees, to take the initiative, crossing boundaries and overcoming barriers, to show God's mercy by serving others.

John tells us many of the Samaritans from Sychar believed in Jesus because of the woman's testimony (see John 4:39). They urged Jesus to stay with them, and He remained in their town for two days. *Two days*. Don't read over that too quickly. We have no information about what Jesus may have said to His disciples during this extended visit. I can imagine the awkwardness the disciples must have felt at staying in a Samaritan home, eating at a Samaritan table, and watching Jesus treat people Jews had despised for centuries with dignity and respect. He validated the Samaritan villagers' spiritual inquisitiveness with the same graceful responses He had shown the woman at the well. They now believed in Him as the Savior of the world, not merely because of the woman's testimony, but because of the words of Jesus Himself (see verse 42).

Don't let the power of that phrase escape you: Savior of the *world*. Not merely Savior of the Jews, but the world, including the mixed-race Samaritans with all their baggage. Jesus was intentionally expanding the worldview of His disciples—open your eyes! But cultural prejudices, impressions on the heart and mind, are like valleys carved over centuries by rivers and not easily traversed. Bias-induced blindness is not quickly cured, as would be evidenced by a later visit to Samaria.

## SAMARITAN OPPOSITION

In Luke 9, just one chapter before the story of the Good Samaritan, the people in a Samaritan village did not welcome Jesus because He was headed for Jerusalem (see verse 53). Their deeply rooted doctrinal disputes led Samaritans to heckle Jews who were en route to Jerusalem to worship in the temple; it was one of the few practices that on occasion led to violence. Two of Jesus' disciples, James and John, aptly named the "Sons of Thunder," wanted to call down fire from heaven to destroy the inhospitable Samaritans (verse 54). Surely they would have remembered the earlier encounter Jesus had in another Samaritan village after meeting the woman at the well. Perhaps James and John felt justified in their "righteous indignation," believing this community of

Samaritans was showing their true colors.

In reading Luke's account of James and John asking Jesus if He would like them "to call down fire from heaven to destroy" a Samaritan village, I am left with a question of my own: Should we admire the fact that James and John had faith strong enough to believe they could reprise the exploits of Elijah to call down fire from heaven? Or should we despise their lack of mercy? Perhaps both. But Jesus would have none of it. He rebuked them and went to another village, also in Samaria. I can't help but wonder if, after finding Samaritan hosts willing to care for their needs, Jesus provided a "refresher" lesson for His disciples, reminding them of their foray into Sychar and the fruit of their ministry there.

## A SURPRISE TWIST

If the disciples, having been challenged by Jesus to see what God sees in a Samaritan village, struggled to show mercy instead of wrath, we can only imagine how difficult it was for a Jewish audience to accept the ethnicity of the hero in the parable of the Good Samaritan. Jesus could have taken a conventional, less controversial approach by making the good guy a Jew and concluding the story by emphasizing how God wants us to show neighborly initiative *even when* we despise those in need. But it would not have had anything close to the emotional impact of the plotline He chose. By making the hero a Samaritan who showed mercy to a Jew, Jesus embedded the truth about serving others, including enemies, in the narrative itself. And in doing so He welded together a lesson for the heart and the head, the will and the emotions.

The antagonistic demeanor of the religious expert who approached Jesus in Luke 10 set the stage for a verbal chess match. He began with a question designed to test Jesus and ended with a question designed to justify himself. The surprise twist Jesus inserted in the story, making the hero a Samaritan, was "check." Turning the question that prompted the story—"Who is my neighbor?"—on its head by asking, "Which of these three do you think was a neighbor to the man?" was "checkmate." But Jesus wasn't teaching a new message. He had already raised the bar above the letter of the Law, challenging true children of God to love their enemies. The Good Samaritan was actually a remedial lesson wrapped in a narrative package.

## JESUS RAISES THE BAR, AGAIN

If someone in the crowd had asked Jesus to expand on the truth behind the parable of the Good Samaritan, He may well have repeated the essence of His radical teaching recorded in Luke 6 about loving your enemies. As if to make sure there would be no question what it looks like to love an enemy, Jesus elaborated, saying, "Do good to those who hate you, bless those who curse you, pray for those who mistreat you" (Luke 6:27-28). This is the essence of taking the initiative to be a neighbor. The "go and do likewise" exhortation in the sequel of the Good Samaritan redefined the neighborhood to include people who are not like you (Samaritans), don't like you, can't repay you, and wouldn't thank you to do so.

Then Jesus raised the bar even higher.

> If you love those who love you, what credit is that to you? Even "sinners" love those who love them. And if you do good to those who are good to you, what credit is that to you? Even "sinners" do that. And if you lend to those from whom you expect repayment, what credit is that to you? Even "sinners" lend to "sinners," expecting to be repaid in full. But love your enemies, do good to them, and lend to them without expecting to get anything back. (Luke 6:32-35)

## YOU WILL NEED GRACE

A common first response to reading these words of Jesus is to search for evidence that justifies our belief that He could not have actually meant what He said. Surely this must be some clever combination of metaphor and hyperbole? Can anyone actually do this? The Samaritan did. And remember the punch line of the sequel, "Go and do likewise." So clearly Jesus expects us to put these radical behaviors into practice. But how?

In this passage Jesus uses a communication technique I describe as rhetorical repetition. Effective communicators often use a rhetorical question to engage listeners, drawing them into the teaching by identifying a point of truth that should be so obvious it can be answered in the minds of the audience. In this teaching Jesus repeats the same rhetorical question three times, "What credit is that to you?" When we see rhetorical questions such as this in the Bible, the simplest way to capture the meaning is to turn the question into a statement that reflects the obvious answer that is being highlighted. In this case, we capture the meaning as follows:

"If you love those who love you, *you won't get any credit for that.* Even 'sinners' love those who love them. And if you do good to those who are good to you, *you won't get any credit for that.* Even 'sinners' do that. And if you lend to those from whom you expect repayment, *you won't get any credit for that.* Even 'sinners' lend to 'sinners' expecting to be repaid in full."

Capturing the meaning in this manner is helpful, but in this passage it can also limit our understanding because of the word *credit*. The original language word here is *charis*, which is usually translated "grace," most notably in Ephesians 2:8: "For it is by grace (*charis*) you have been saved, through faith." Literally, what Jesus is saying here is, "If you love those who love you, you won't get any *charis* for that." The word *charis* can mean "to thank," which is how it is translated in the King James Version of the Bible. But what if the full range of meaning associated with *charis* is in order here, both thanks and grace? "If you love those who love you, you won't get any thanks or grace for that."

To capture the full meaning of this teaching, we need to go one step further, turning the negative into a positive, as follows:

"If you love those who don't love you, *you will receive grace for that.* And if you do good to those who are not good to you, *you will receive grace for that.* And if you lend to those from whom you don't expect repayment, *you will receive grace for that.*"

How can anyone possibly live out this truth in a redefined neighborhood that includes people who are not like me, don't like me, can't repay me, and probably won't thank me? How can we practice the central truth of the Good Samaritan, taking initiative to overcome barriers and cross boundaries to show God's mercy by serving others? You will need grace for that.

## TAKE MY COAT TOO

Jesus has radically redefined the neighborhood, not just for first-century religious experts, but for all of us. It includes people who aren't like us, don't like us, can't repay us, and won't thank us. What does this look like in real life? I can't think of a better example than the unusual evening commute of Julio Diaz. You may remember hearing his story, as told on National Public Radio.

Like most of us, Julio Diaz is a creature of habit. The thirty-one-year-old social worker ends his hour-long subway commute on the Number 6 train to the Bronx one stop early every night so he can enjoy a meal at his favorite diner. But his routine took an unexpected turn on the platform one evening as he walked toward the stairs. A teenage boy approached Julio, pulled out a knife, and asked for his money.

With a combination of street smarts and survival skills, Julio handed over his wallet. If the story ended here, it would be unfortunate and unremarkable. But just as for Julio Diaz, this teenage burglar's evening was about to take an unexpected turn. As he walked away, wallet in hand, Julio called out to his attacker.

"Hey, wait a minute. You forgot something. If you're going to be robbing people for the rest of the night, you might as well take my coat to keep you warm."[2]

Surprised and suspicious, the teen asked his victim, "Why are you doing this?" Julio replied: "If you're willing to risk your freedom for a few dollars, then I guess you must really need the money. I mean, all I wanted to do was get dinner and if you really want to join me . . . hey, you're more than welcome."[3]

With that invitation, a most unusual duo walked out of the subway to the diner. Because Julio eats at this location almost every day after work, he was greeted cordially by everyone from waiters to dishwashers, including the manager. His unlikely dinner guest was surprised and confused by the friendships Julio had formed with such an eclectic mix of people at the diner. As they talked over a meal, Julio asked the teen what he really wanted out of life, but his only response was a solemn and sad stare into space.

As they finished eating, the bill arrived. Julio pointed out that he had no money and suggested if the teen returned the wallet, dinner would be on him. Without even thinking about it, the teen returned Julio's wallet. In addition to dinner, Julio gave his new acquaintance $20, asking for something in return—the teen's knife, which he also handed over.

Julio summed up the experience, saying, "I figure, you know, if you treat people right, you can only hope that they treat you right. It's as simple as it gets in this complicated world."[4]

I believe it takes more than courage to do what Julio Diaz did. You will need grace for that. And I believe God wants to give it to you.

## THE HOOD GETS BIGGER, THE WORLD GETS SMALLER

Take a moment to think about the scope and the scale of what Jesus is really teaching us here.

In redefining the neighborhood, Jesus erased the logical barriers we construct in our minds and hearts to keep out the people we have been culturally preconditioned to exclude from neighborly initiatives. He has made the neighborhood in which Good Samaritan activities should play out bigger than it was before. As He did with the disciples in Samaria, Jesus is exhorting us—"Open your eyes!"

But while the hood is getting bigger, the world is getting smaller. Many of the people who aren't like me, don't like me, won't thank me, and couldn't repay me live far away from me. In Jesus' day, I may not even have known they existed. And should they experience difficulty, the equivalent of being left for dead along the side of the road, it is very unlikely I would have ever heard about it at all. But we don't live in that world. It has changed . . . forever. The impact of globalization makes the world smaller, and the redefinition of the neighborhood makes the world bigger. These two forces are converging upon us, demanding more intentional reflection on how to balance the demands of loving a mugger in America and a mullah in Afghanistan, between showing mercy to a needy person at the exit ramp on my commute home from work and an earthquake victim in Haiti, between Eutisha Rennix and Bant Singh.

How do we prevent better information about what is happening in the world from becoming burdensome information that overwhelms us, stifling rather than empowering action? We'll focus our attention on that important question in part 2, exploring how to work together with God to transform a flood of information into rivers of passion that fuel a purposeful life. But before we turn that corner, there are a few more lessons and observations we can extrapolate from the story of the Good Samaritan.

# Chapter 3

# FROM INFORMATION TO ACTION

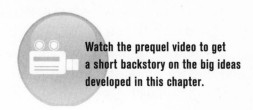

Watch the prequel video to get
a short backstory on the big ideas
developed in this chapter.

Cannibals want missionaries.

Those three words on a promotional flyer in Liverpool, England, captured the imagination of C. T. Studd. C. T. had served as a missionary in both China and India, and his curiosity was duly piqued upon reading this creatively worded advertisement. He had to go in. Once inside the meeting, he heard Dr. Karl Kumm share about the desperate needs in the heart of Africa. The big-game hunters, mapmakers, merchants, and explorers had gone; but no one had gone for the cause of Christ. And millions of people were still waiting for their first chance to hear the gospel message.

C. T. Studd was an unlikely candidate for pioneer service of this nature. He was fifty years old and had returned to England due to failing health after serving in India for fifteen years. But the information he heard in that meeting seeped into his heart like soaking rain on parched soil. Information gave birth to compassion that demanded action.

He wrote about that night, describing the feelings he had upon hearing of the great need:

"The shame sank deep into one's soul. I said, 'Why have no Christians gone?' God replied, 'Why don't you go?' 'The doctors won't permit it,' I said. The answer came, 'Am I not the Good Physician? Can I not take you through? Can I not keep you there?' There were no excuses, it had to be done."[1]

At this unlikely moment in the journey, a new sense of responsibility for the needs of others was taking shape. But it would require sacrificial obedience. C. T. had no money. He was not up to the challenges physically. How could he survive in tropical Africa? And what mission organization would send him?

A group of businessmen formed a committee to back the venture, on one condition—C. T. must receive the clearance of a doctor. The doctor's report was dead set against C. T. Studd's participation in this project. He responded to the committee, saying, "Gentlemen, God has called me to go, and I will go. I will blaze a trail, though my grave may only become a stepping stone that younger men may follow."[2] C. T. Studd did die in Africa, more than twenty years later, after founding a new mission society called the Heart of Africa Mission, today WEC International.

## PRINCIPLE AND PATTERN

C. T. Studd's response to what he learned about the heart of Africa that night in Liverpool clearly reflects the single thought, the one overarching principle Jesus communicated in the story of the Good Samaritan. God expects us to take initiative in crossing boundaries and overcoming barriers to show His mercy by serving others. How you respond to the needs of others depends on who you love the most. If you love God first, you will live others-focused. But his story also mirrors a pattern modeled by Jesus and reflected in the story of the Good Samaritan. It is a pattern you have likely experienced in your own journey:

Information leads to compassion.

Compassion demands action.

"But a Samaritan, as he traveled, came where the man was; and when he *saw him*, he *took pity on him*. He *went to him*" (Luke 10:33-34).

| "he saw him" | "he took pity on him" | "he went to him" |
|---|---|---|
| - - - - - - - - - - - - - - - - - - - - - - - - - - - - - - - - - - → | | |
| information | compassion | action |

In this progression the Samaritan man is giving us a visual answer to the question, "What would Jesus do?" Repeatedly in His public ministry Jesus operated in this same pattern. He saw people in need, was moved with compassion, and took practical action. After hearing the news of John the Baptist's beheading, Jesus wanted some time alone to mourn the death of His friend. So Jesus "withdrew by boat privately to a solitary place." Yet even in this time of personal sorrow, "When Jesus landed and saw a large crowd, he had compassion on them and healed their sick" (Matthew 14:14).

## PREACTION EXIT RAMPS

The story of the Good Samaritan explicitly states all three men traveling from Jerusalem to Jericho—the priest, Levite, and Samaritan—saw the man left for dead on the side of the road. In this setting they literally fixed their eyes on him. But the original language word translated "saw" can also mean "to be aware of." It would be foolish to limit the sense of responsibility we have in serving others to those who actually fall in our field of view, as if somehow literally turning our back on the needy exonerates us. We'll revisit this issue later in the chapter, specifically focusing on how globalization complicates this part of the process. For now, suffice it to say, the first stage in the pattern is information: "He saw him."

The New International Version describes the Samaritan's response to the information about the wounded traveler, saying, "He took pity on him." The original-language word here is almost always translated as "compassion." When Jesus is described as being moved with compassion, it is the same Greek word used here in the story of the Good Samaritan (see Matthew 14:14; 15:32; 20:34). Literally the phrase means "to have the bowels yearn." Today we might describe it as a "gut-wrenching" experience. Awareness of the need, information ("he saw him") produced compassion ("he took pity on him)," which resulted in practical action ("he went to him)."

This is how it is supposed to work. But we all understand what should be is not always what is. In between compassion and action there are some common exit ramps. I describe them as intention, deflection, rationalization, and justification. While these exit ramps do not flow directly from the teaching of the Good Samaritan, I think you will agree they help explain why and how we are so easily sidetracked somewhere between compassion and action. They give us a grid for understanding the behavior of the priest and Levite.

## Exit 1—Intention

More often than I'd like to admit, I have been made aware of a specific need, felt the compassion of God aroused within my spirit, and affirmed the good intention to take practical action based on the hope I could make a difference. *I really ought to write her a note of encouragement. I really ought to call to pray with him about that need. I really ought to give to help advance that cause.* I mean well. Really.

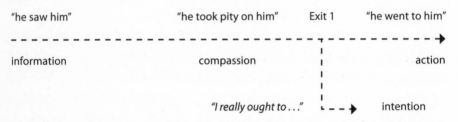

But it is too easy for my good intentions to get swallowed up by the harried and hurried pace of life. If I don't forget about what I felt I really ought to do, I often find myself procrastinating until it seems as if the window of opportunity is lost. There is almost always a moment of regret when I come to believe I've missed a chance to let information about the needs of others produce compassionate action. But I've noticed a scary temptation that may be even *more* troublesome than my failure to act: ascribing spiritual merit for merely having the intention to do something even if I don't follow through.

The mental gymnastics go something like this: *Well, at least I thought about doing something. I'm sure there were plenty of people who learned about that need and never intended to do anything. After all, it's the thought that counts.*

No, it isn't.

The thought only counts when it reflects untarnished motives contrasted with unskilled action. Imagine a child trampling through a beautiful flower garden in the backyard to pick a bouquet for his grandmother. He comes in the back door with a handful of flowers behind his back and hollers with excitement for his "Nana." As she walks in the kitchen, with great pride and joy he thrusts the flowers toward her, saying, "I picked these for you, Nana!"

A wise grandmother will at least for the moment overlook the dirt tracked in from the flower garden, accept the bouquet, put it in a vase on the counter, and express her wild appreciation for this act of love and generosity. Only later will she offer gentle and loving remedial instruction about the flower garden. Why? Because in this case, untarnished motives are contrasted with unskilled action. In this case, it *is* the thought that counts.

When we assign ourselves spiritual merit for merely thinking about serving others, we are vulnerable to a dangerous form of hypocrisy that is difficult to confront because the self-righteousness is dressed up in good intentions. We view ourselves as active participants in the life of the body when others know we are merely passive observers. This is a self-awareness gap. We think we are mature, balancing knowledge with obedience, but we are not. The merit we are assigning to ourselves based on good intentions is invisible. This is stealth hypocrisy. We become the fools who, after looking at ourselves in the mirror, walk away, immediately forgetting what we look like. We are hearers only; good intenders, but not doers (see James 1:22-25).

For almost seventy-five years the Ad Council has sought to stir people to action with public service announcements. One of my personal favorites is the "Don't Almost Give" campaign. One ad shows a man with crutches struggling to go up a flight of concrete stairs. The narrator says, "This is a man who almost learned to walk at a rehab center that almost got built by people who almost gave money." After a brief pause, the announcer continues: "Almost gave. How good is *almost* giving? About as good as *almost* walking."

Another ad shows an older woman sitting alone in a room, staring out a window. The narrator says, "This is Sarah Watkins. A lot of people almost helped her. One almost cooked for her. Another almost drove her to the doctor. Still another almost stopped by to say hello. They *almost* helped. They *almost* gave of themselves. But *almost* giving is the same as not giving at all."

 That's true, regardless of your intentions.

## Exit 2—Deflection

At some point in your spiritual journey, you have probably found yourself listening to a powerful teaching that triggers the following thought: *This is really good stuff; I hope my spouse (or child or friend or whomever) is paying attention.* Similarly, you have probably been exposed to information about the needs of others and reacted by looking at the people around you, saying, "Aren't you going to do something about that?" I call this deflection.

There is a difference between mobilization—seeking to rally a greater number of people to engage in a legitimate cause—and deflection. Mobilization is a legitimate expression of action, while deflection is an exit ramp that allows us to avoid taking action in a manner that minimizes the risk of exposure by turning the attention away from ourselves and shining the spotlight on others. Some people have perfected this craft. They speak with a sense of righteous indignation, "Why don't you do something about that?"

Perhaps one of the most powerful laboratories in which we perfect the art of deflection is at home. We see a mess that needs to be cleaned up, and we deflect responsibility for dealing with it to someone else. We know each other so well that a mere glance says it all: *Aren't you going to do something about that?* In my family it's not really fair because my wife and kids know my obsession for order and neatness makes it nearly impossible for me to resist cleaning up a mess when I see it. I'm not more spiritual; I'm more dysfunctional.

Deflection is often followed by hypothetical declarations such as "If I had known about her need, I would have stepped up to take Mrs. Watkins a meal, take her to the doctor, and get her prescription filled." This overlaps with Exit 1—Intentions, in that it allows us to claim spiritual merit for action *we did not take* in the past. It is retroactive good intentions. People who brag about what they are going to do tomorrow probably said the same thing yesterday. People who brag about what they would have done yesterday will probably say the same thing tomorrow.

Jesus called out this kind of hypocrisy in the Pharisees, who were padding their coffers of self-righteousness by bragging about what they would not have done in the past. Jesus exposed their foolishness, saying, "And you say, 'If we had lived in the days of our forefathers, we would not have taken part with them in shedding the blood of the prophets.'" They tried to distance themselves from the murderous behavior of their forefathers when in reality they were seeking to take the same action against Jesus. No wonder he called them "snakes," a "brood of vipers!" (see Matthew 23:30-33).

When faced with information about the needs of others that is incontrovertible, for which we don't want to become responsible, a common exit ramp is deflection, the art of turning the spotlight of attention on someone else.

## Exit 3—Rationalization

Regardless of how gifted, resourced, or networked one might be, it is impossible for anyone to do everything. But rationalization is not about the discipline needed to create margin or the focus required to be decisive. Rationalization has a ring of defensiveness that tries to explain why a need that clearly could have been met is not, why someone failed to take the initiative to show God's mercy by serving others. In rationalizing we say things such as "It will take hundreds of millions of dollars to rebuild Haiti; the $25 I had to contribute won't be missed." We never stop to think about the fact that a million other people probably said the same thing.

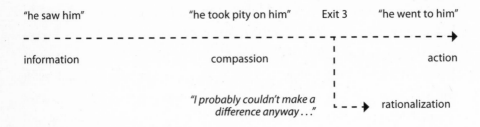

Rationalization is more an excuse than an explanation. I'm too busy to volunteer, but I have plenty of time for March Madness. I can't afford to give to that worthy cause, but I seem to be able to find the cash for my triple grande, nonfat, no whip, no foam, extra hot white mocha whenever I pass a Starbucks. It's amazing how financial self-control and the discipline of time management rise up when people are invited to give or volunteer for a worthy cause and melt like ice cream on a hot summer day when faced with a sale on big-screen televisions.

## Exit 4—Justification

While rationalization has a ring of defensiveness, justification adds a sense of superiority. It suggests that if you knew what I know or had the experiences I've had, you would understand and support my decision not to take action in response to this need. In some cases this air of superiority goes so far as to suggest, "I'm so far ahead of you that you wouldn't get it even if I tried to explain it to you." "I have my reasons." There are times our attempts to help actually hurt those in need. But people who know the difference simply find a better way to help rather than sitting smugly on the sidelines.

In some ways justification is deflection and rationalization on steroids. It leads us to faulty conclusions such as all poor people are lazy and giving to them would only reward their lack of effort. It suggests HIV/AIDS is a lifestyle disease and most of the people infected brought it on themselves, as if their poor choices have disqualified them from God's mercy. And then there is the mother of all justification trump cards that categorizes everything from natural disasters to oppressive governments as "divine judgment," as if to say helping suffering people unfortunate enough to find themselves in this setting would be tantamount to opposing God. As long as a person clings to beliefs of this nature, it is easy to justify inaction and the sense of superiority over others who are either too naive or too simple-minded to agree with him.

## EXEMPTION DETOUR

I have placed these four exit ramps between compassion and action. But if we take them often enough, there is a danger of bypassing compassion altogether, taking a detour of the heart that speedily routes us to the exit ramp destination of choice. I label this detour "exemption." Taking it often suggests we are exempting ourselves from the careful process of assessing what God might want us to do in response to a given need. Perhaps this is why the priest and Levite in the story of the Good Samaritan "saw the man" beaten and left for dead but "passed by on the other side" (Luke 10:31-32). They both had information about the need, but there is not even a hint of compassion and there is a complete lack of action.

"he saw him"          "he took pity on him"          "he went to him"

information          compassion          action

Exemption Detour          intention
deflection
rationalization
justification

I think you can see by now that it is one thing to be aware of a need, to have information, to feel a measure of compassion rise up in your spirit, and something else altogether to take practical action. The Good Samaritan shows us how it is supposed to work, what Jesus would do. But there is a vast wasteland of missed opportunities, of almost serving, in between compassion and action. The priest and the Levite remind us that a godly heritage and spiritual training do not automatically translate into Christlike initiative in the service of others. In their decision to pass by on the other side, we have a warning of the danger of creating a detour around compassion, avoiding any possible gut-wrenching experiences in our hurry to find solace in our favorite exit ramp.

This is true when the measure of responsibility for serving others is limited to *physical* proximity plus urgency plus capacity. It is even more complicated when we add *virtual* proximity, or proximity to the power of Google, which adds the flood of information about the urgent needs of others I am aware of because they are virtually, but not physically, close to me.

As the world becomes virtually smaller and the flow of information literally faster, there is even more pressure to take an exit ramp on the way to practical action or the detour that bypasses compassion altogether. You might remember the story of Neda, a twenty-seven-year-old music student from Iran who participated in demonstrations in Tehran in the summer of 2009. Caught in the cross fire of this political unrest, Neda became the symbol of the opposition movement. Amateur video footage of her lying in a pool of her own blood, breathing her final breaths, was posted on Twitter feeds, YouTube, and ultimately broadcast on news channels around the world.

The untimely death of a young student with a promising future would be tragic no matter when it happened. But for most of the history of the world it would have been hidden from everyone without physical proximity to the tragedy. When the needs of the world are on display in real time, physical proximity is expanded by virtual proximity that can result in information overload and compassion fatigue.

## INFORMATION OVERLOAD–COMPASSION FATIGUE

The picture I'm painting for you is not intended to pile on new levels of guilt and shame. I'm trying to help you come to terms with the reality of how complicated a simple question such as "Who is my neighbor?" has become in this globalized world. I'm trying to give some shape and contour to the emotions and decisions we face as we try to make sense of our God-given responsibility to take the initiative in crossing boundaries and overcoming barriers to show God's mercy by serving others.

| "he saw him and her" | "he felt burned out" | "he almost acted" |
|---|---|---|
| information overload | compassion fatigue | inaction |

The problem we are wrestling with is not the lack of information about the needs of others. It is information overload, which too often produces pseudo-compassion fatigue. To modify the wording of the Good

Samaritan, we could say, "He saw him and her and him and her, and he was overwhelmed, almost burned out, to the point where he felt paralyzed and didn't take action." In clinical jargon, true compassion fatigue is referred to as Secondary Traumatic Stress Disorder (STSD). Symptoms of STSD include anxiety, lack of productivity, negative attitudes, and diminished capacity for empathy, usually resulting from repeated and extended exposure to and service among victims of trauma.

In recent years compassion fatigue has been offered as an explanation for the diminished interest and generosity people feel toward those in need after too much exposure to too many disasters in too short a period of time. The 2004 tsunami resulting from the earthquake in the Indian Ocean generated a global response. But other natural disasters following the tsunami did not trigger the level of interest we might have expected if they occurred the year before. The 2010 earthquake in Chile would likely have received more coverage and greater response had it not occurred so soon after the earthquake in Haiti. No doubt the scope of the problem in Haiti was much larger than the situation in Chile, and the capacity of relief and development organizations was already stretched to the limit. But it seems clear compassion fatigue played a role in the amount of coverage and response to the needs in Chile.

As the world continues to get smaller and communication continues to get faster, we are in danger of producing a society that lives in chronic pseudo-compassion fatigue. I say pseudo-compassion fatigue because it does not result from the traditional caregiver experience of giving too much without taking time to refuel. It is the result of too much almost giving, almost serving.

But it doesn't have to be this way.

## PASSION-PRIORITIZED ACTION

In part 1 of this book I've been focused on the lessons we learn from the Good Samaritan and how they apply to our increasingly complicated and globalized world. In part 2 we'll turn our attention to a pathway that will enable you to organize and prioritize your service of others, mitigating information overload and compassion fatigue. The word *compassion* comes from Latin and means "with passion," or more literally, "together suffering." The pattern observed in the life of Jesus and illustrated by the Good Samaritan is information, awareness of the needs of others, produces compassion, which leads to action. It is a picture of together suffering. I believe if you let God lead you on this journey of together suffering, you will emerge with passion. And your passion will give you direction; it will enable you to calibrate responsibility for serving others with whom you have physical or virtual proximity.

God can use life-shaping experiences such as the short-term mission trip you took last year or the powerful message you heard last month or the news story you will hear tonight on your drive home or the meeting C. T. Studd attended in Liverpool to transform the ocean of information regarding the needs of others into rivers of passion that fuel Spirit-directed action. I want to show you how.

# Part 2

# CONNECTING WITH YOUR PASSIONS

Chapter 4

# TWO STREAMS OF PASSION

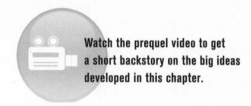

Watch the prequel video to get a short backstory on the big ideas developed in this chapter.

In the spring of 1884, a seventeen-year-old Irish girl named Amy went to a Belfast tea shop with her mother. While sipping tea and nibbling sweet delicacies she noticed a young girl standing outside with her face pressed against the window of the tea shop. Amy found it charming and amusing to observe the little girl's perusal of tantalizing sweets on display in the window. But the innocence of that moment was about to be interrupted.

As she walked out the door with her mother, Amy's gaze playfully returned to the little girl. There she stood, barefoot, dirty, wearing a thin and ragged dress in the light rain. Without a word being spoken, in a matter of seconds, Amy's perspective on the situation changed. The eyes of her heart were opened. In the words of the Good Samaritan, she "saw her." The little girl's poverty was anything but charming. Compassion was aroused in Amy's spirit.

Later that evening, in the warmth and comfort of her own bedroom, Amy reflected on this experience and wrote, "When I grow up and money have, I know what I will do, I'll build a great big lovely place for little girls like you."[1] Then in a moment of honest self-reflection, Amy continued writing, "And yet at present I do nothing 'for little girls like you.' Please, God, tell me what to do."[2]

Seventeen-year-old Amy Carmichael was being impressed by the Holy Spirit to take the initiative in crossing boundaries and overcoming barriers to show God's mercy by serving others. She had a Good Samaritan experience on the side of the road by a tea shop in Belfast. There were other people who passed by this little girl, but they did not see what Amy saw. Information was triggering compassion that would soon be translated into action. All of this together would eventually help refine Amy's passion for the marginalized, exploited, and underserved.

We'll revisit Amy's story later in this chapter, but first I want to make the connection between Google and the Good Samaritan, between hyperlinks and "heartlinks."

## PAGERANK AND PASSION

Google is one of the most powerful and visible icons of globalization. Riding the wave of increased bandwidth and mobile connectivity, search engines such as Google have done more to democratize information than anything since Gutenberg invented the printing press. If a schoolgirl in Mumbai and a scholar in Oxford both want to know the gross domestic product (GDP) of Mozambique, the only difference between them is the connection speed of the Internet café in India compared to the bandwidth at the university in England. In a matter of seconds, if the connection speed is slow, nanoseconds if it's fast, they both have access to more information than anyone could possibly have imagined even a few decades ago.

To prove my point, I just typed "GDP of Mozambique" into the Google search bar on my computer, and in a fraction of a second I discovered as of June 2010, according to the U.S. Department of State, it is $17.64 billion. I chose this search topic at random to illustrate the power of PageRank, the trademarked and patented link analysis algorithm named after Larry Page, the cofounder of Google. According to Wikipedia, PageRank "assigns a numerical weighting to each element of a hyperlinked set of documents . . . with the purpose of 'measuring' its relative importance within the set."[3] Here's how Google explains it on its corporate website:

The software behind our search technology conducts a series of simultaneous calculations requiring only a fraction of a second. Traditional search engines rely heavily on how often a word appears on a web page. We use more than two hundred signals, including our patented PageRank™ algorithm, to examine the entire link structure of the web and determine which pages are most important. We then conduct hypertext-matching analysis to determine which pages are relevant to the specific search being conducted. By combining overall importance and query-specific relevance, we're able to put the most relevant and reliable results first.[4]

I can't really explain all that to you in plain English. But what I do understand is PageRank enables Google to translate a few key words such as "GDP of Mozambique" into a list of hyperlinks with "the most relevant and reliable results first." It shakes down the thousands of different sources of information and pulls together an algorithmically calculated list of data points with the most important ones at the top of the page. Regardless of whether you can spell Mozambique (Google can) or find it on a map, you can confirm the GDP in a few nanoseconds.

Factoids aside, what does Google have to do with the Good Samaritan?

What if there was a functional equivalent of PageRank for sorting out the answer to the question, "Who is my neighbor?" What if the same tools that supercharge globalization could actually point the way forward for us as we try to make sense of our response to the needs of others? What if we could borrow a page from Larry Page and generate a PageRank of our own that helps focus our primary service of others around God-ordained passions?

What if this is how you find your neighbor?

I believe God uses life-shaping experiences, as subtle and unexpected as Amy's encounter with a little girl outside a tea shop in Belfast, to create "heartlinks" that, like hyperlinks in Google's PageRank, become part of a spiritual algorithm, organizing and prioritizing the passions that connect us with opportunities for meaningful service. Identifying these passions and creating your own heartlink-driven PageRank will enable you to sort through the many opportunities a globalized world presents to find the few God-ordained places for you to leverage your giftedness to make a lasting impact. This is how the ocean of information can become rivers of passion, how you can move from being tossed back and forth by waves to flowing with the current toward a meaningful future.

## BACK TO BELFAST

Several weeks after the heartlink at the tea shop, while walking home from the Rosemary Street Presbyterian Church, Amy saw an elderly woman struggling to carry a heavy bundle. She impulsively urged her two brothers, Norman and Ernest, to join her in helping the woman. One of her brothers took the woman's bundle, while the other supported an arm on the opposite side of the woman from Amy. As they walked, the streets became increasingly busy with pedestrians headed home from other churches. Amy couldn't help but notice the people were staring at them. She became increasingly self-conscious. Surely these people couldn't assume she knew this woman? In a moment, compassionate action morphed into prideful self-absorption, childish embarrassment, and fickle self-consciousness.

In Amy's mind this good deed had become "a horrid moment." As they passed an ornate Victorian fountain in the street, "This mighty phrase flashed as it were through the gray drizzle: 'Gold, silver, precious stones, wood, hay, stubble—every man's work will be made manifest; for the day shall declare it, because it will be tested by fire; and the fire shall try every man's work of what sort it is. If any man's work abide. . . .'"[5]

The words rang out like a thunderclap. Amy turned to see who had spoken them. She saw nothing but the muddy streets and the fountain. Norman and Ernest heard nothing. But Amy knew this was the voice of God. Later that afternoon, Amy Carmichael shut herself in her room. She realized God was asking for her "gold" and was mortified with embarrassment that she had offered Him only "stubble." She prayed, "Oh God, let me serve you with gold."[6]

With heart humbled and motives purified, Amy was drawn back to the heartlink established on the sidewalk outside the tea shop. It was time to translate the compassion she felt for the little girl into action. Amy began by inviting the children of her neighborhood to gather at her house on Sunday afternoons to play games, sing songs, and listen to Bible stories. As much as Amy enjoyed sharing with the neighborhood children, she realized there were others who had much less of a chance to hear the good news. She volunteered at the Belfast City Mission and visited the slums with the Reverend Henry Montgomery. Soon Amy was working with the poorest of her community, holding groups for both boys and girls.

Eventually some older girls were drawn to her meetings. They worked in the mills and could not afford the proper hats of the day. They covered their heads with shawls and were commonly referred to as "shawlies." The mill girls or shawlies were social outcasts. In some cases they were sexually molested. Many of them had become single mothers. Amy invited them to the Rosemary Street church, where she taught them etiquette, hygiene, and, of course, the Bible. The group grew in size to the point they could no longer fit in the Rosemary Street church. Amy needed a place of her own. But at age seventeen, how could she ever afford it?

Over lunch one day, Amy shared her desire for a building with Kate Mitchell, a wealthy matron in the community. In a matter of days Amy received five hundred pounds from Kate Mitchell, along with a note saying, "Build your hall." A mill owner donated the land, and on January 2, 1889, the "Welcome Hall," as Amy called it, was dedicated. She was offering God her gold, and He was refining her passions, ordering the PageRank of her heartlinks and preparing Amy for future appointments with destiny that would leverage her giftedness in the service of others.

I believe you have heartlinks like this too. And there are more waiting for you in the future. I want to help you understand why these life-shaping experiences are so important and how they develop into passions that fuel a life of meaningful service. Keep in mind that Amy Carmichael started on this journey as a teenager only a matter of weeks after surrendering her heart to Jesus. This is not reserved for vocational ministry leaders or an elite class of superspiritual Christ followers.

## TWO STREAMS OF PASSION

There are two streams of passion potential in all of us. Both streams flow from self-directed sources of motivation. If you are truly passionate about something, you won't need others to drive you to pursue it. The first stream is your interest-based passions, things you do for fun that bring you pleasure. The second stream is your issue-based passions, activities you find fulfilling that give you a sense of purpose. Passion, both interest- and issue-based, is rarely ever produced in a vacuum. Don't expect a randomly occurring spontaneous combustion of passion that instantly PageRanks and prioritizes the opportunities available to realize your potential and make a difference in the lives of others.

My observation and experience suggest interest-based passions form when ability (or aptitude) and opportunity converge. Some people are passionate about chess, others baseball, still others handicrafts, and so on. We tend to like what we are good at and be good at what we like. Ability, or at least potential, and opportunity must be present for interest-based passions to develop, though some personalities are more inclined than others to create opportunities where they might otherwise not exist. In using the word *fun* to describe interest-based passions, I don't mean frivolous. Many interest-based passions are meaningful and rewarding, with a measure of stand-alone value, but not on the same scale with the causes on which one's purpose or legacy is built.

Issue-based passions develop at the intersection of experience and empathy, what I've labeled heartlinks. If you talk to someone who is passionate about homelessness or sex trafficking or AIDS orphans, you will discover, somewhere in his or her journey, one or more meaningful experiences that unearthed a heightened level of empathy, the headwaters for a stream of issue-based passion. These heartlinks of passion are used by God to provide information that arouses compassion and translates into some kind of action. For Amy Carmichael it started rather unexpectedly as a teenager outside a tea shop in Belfast. For C. T. Studd it began inside a meeting hall in Liverpool at age fifty.[7] If you can articulate your own issue-based passion, you probably recall where your journey began. If you can't, the heartlink that opens the headwaters of informed, compassionate action could be just around the corner.

## THE PASSION PYRAMID

A hallmark of passion, whether interest- or issue-based, is an inner source of motivation and self-directed initiative. Passionate people benefit like everyone else from cheerleaders who believe in them and partners who hold them accountable. But if you are truly passionate you will not need to be cajoled or corralled into action. Passion is evidenced by self-directed initiative to learn more about, engage in, and influence others toward interests and issues even when sacrifice is required. I describe this progression of self-directed learning, engaging, influencing, and sacrificing as the passion pyramid.

At the base of the passion pyramid is self-directed motivation to learn more about an interest or issue. Depending on how meaningful the experience that triggered the heartlink, this quest for information can be almost insatiable, prodding us to explore a variety of resources ranging from Internet searches to articles, books, YouTube videos, as well as formal and informal training opportunities. The second level in the passion pyramid involves some kind of participatory engagement. We continue our learning by some form of doing. We engage in activities we believe will meet a need, right a wrong, solve a problem, or promote a cause. The participation ranges from practicing a newly developing interest to engaging with an important issue by giving, volunteering, or taking other meaningful action.

The third level in the passion pyramid is influencing others toward the interest or issue. As we learn more about and begin to engage in our passions, we can't help but enlist others to join us. Passion is contagious. In fact, one of the common heartlinks for passion is creative interaction with another person whose life is overflowing with energy and commitment to an interest or issue.

At the top of the passion pyramid is a willingness to learn, participate, and influence even when it requires us to sacrifice time, energy, money, or personal convenience. Historically passion has always been associated with suffering in one way or another. This connotation for the word *passion* was framed in part by the translators of the King James Bible. The single place these translators chose to use the English word *passion* is Acts 1:3: "To whom also he [Jesus] shewed himself alive after his passion by many infallible proofs, being seen of them forty days, and speaking of the things pertaining to the kingdom of God." From this verse, we have come to associate the passion of Christ with the final hours of suffering He endured from the Last Supper through the Crucifixion. Of the forty times this Greek word, *pascho*, is used in the New Testament, all but three of them are translated "suffer" in the King James.[8]

Genuine passion produces a self-directed commitment to learn more about, participate in, and influence others toward interests or issues even when it requires, as in the case of Christ, sacrifice or suffering.

## EVERYDAY PASSIONS

Once you understand the passion pyramid you will start to recognize the inklings of interest and issue-based passions in yourself and others. My son Josiah has become an interesting case study for me on this topic. As I was preparing to write this chapter, I had a conversation with Josiah on the way home from school. He had been given a special part in the closing act of a drama presentation because of his interest-based passion for yo-yos, and it sparked a conversation about the passion pyramid using his journey as a case study.

Several years ago he became fascinated with yo-yos. Without any outside prodding, Josiah began an obsessive, self-directed journey to learn more about them. He watched YouTube videos and read online forums to help improve his skills. He literally begged my wife and me for odd jobs he could do to earn enough money to buy fancier yo-yos, some of which cost over $100. Eventually he had such an impressive collection of yo-yos that he asked for a special carrying case for Christmas. He practiced for hours, refining high-level tricks. The more Josiah demonstrated his mad yo-yo skills for kids in the neighborhood, the more his friends were influenced to purchase yo-yos of their own. Eventually he entered himself in a state competition, where he came in third place for his age group. On the heels of this positive experience, Josiah posted videos of himself on YouTube and contacted a company to explore its interest in sponsoring him for future competitions. When the company expressed its desire for a sponsorship, Josiah was faced with a much greater level of commitment. He ultimately decided to remain an amateur yo-yo trickster and began to slowly reduce the amount of time and energy invested. This is interest-based passion at work.

With the passion pyramid as a frame of reference, Josiah began discussing a possible issue-based passion he is exploring in the field of medicine. He explained that if he doesn't get a job in the first few weeks of summer, which is probable given the fact he is only fifteen and the job market is tight, he plans to volunteer at a local hospital. I asked why he wanted to volunteer, and he said the medical schools he has investigated online give priority to applicants who have volunteer experience at a hospital. When I suggested he consider a hospital closer to our home for convenience, he told me that wasn't possible; he had already checked the application requirements, and the closer hospitals have a minimum age of sixteen. All of this learning and initial steps toward participating were self-directed. This is what passion looks like in everyday life.

We went on to process the fact that unlike personality or strengths, passion is not hard-wired by your genetics and often changes over time. I told him it doesn't really matter if he ends up in the medical field and there is no reason to put pressure on himself so early in the journey. But the best way to evaluate and refine a possible passion is to learn more about it and explore options for participatory engagement, which is exactly what he was doing by volunteering. If this really is an issue-based passion, over time he will hardly be able to keep from influencing others and will be increasingly open to keep learning as well as engaging even when sacrifice is required. And if medicine is in his future, there will be lots of learning and lots of sacrificing.

## FROM IRELAND TO INDIA

Amy Carmichael's issue-based passion for the vulnerable, marginalized, and outcasts of her community led her from Ireland to India, where she would serve for more than fifty years. But the heartlink established outside the tea shop in Belfast would resurface as unexpectedly as it was established and PageRank the passion that became the cornerstone of her legacy.

A little more than a decade after dedicating the "Welcome Hall" in Belfast, Amy would meet Preena, her first *devadasi* or "temple child," or more literally, "female slave of the deity." Throughout India young girls were sold by their parents to temple priests who initiated them as *devadasis*. Considered married to the temple deities, these young girls were taught ritual dances. In many cases they led a life of religiously sanctioned prostitution. Amy had already established a heartlink with "shawlies" in Ireland; another unexpected life-shaping experience was about to recalibrate the PageRank of Amy's passion, organizing and prioritizing her ministry.

Preena had run away from the temple for a second time. Her hands were scarred from the burns she had been given as punishment for the earlier escape. Amy held the little girl tight. Preena called her

"Amma"—mother. It was a foreshadowing of what was to come. Amy would become a "mother" to forsaken children. "Amma" had been a cry of destiny.

Amy remembered the little girl she had seen outside the Belfast tea shop and the short verse she had written that night. Having been prepared by God through her work with the "shawlies," the time had come to build a place for the Indian version of "little girls like you." That place became known as the Dohnavur Fellowship and is still active in India today. Amy's issue-based passion fueled a long and difficult journey devoted to changing the laws in India so as to protect thousands of future Preenas from this kind of servitude.

## FROM SURRENDER TO ADVENTURE

In reading Amy's story you may have found yourself wondering, *Why don't I ever have experiences like that?* You may have asked this question more than once after interacting with a friend whose life seems to be rich with meaning and filled with passion. I believe everyone has the potential for a passion-filled life. Identifying your passions and pursuing them will enable you to begin to prioritize opportunities for service, which in turn will help protect you from information overload and compassion fatigue. Your journey as a Good Samaritan, taking the initiative to cross boundaries and overcome barriers to show God's mercy by serving others, will be streamlined by the heartlinks that connect you with your passions. You can't force a life-shaping experience such as Amy's on the doorstep of the tea shop or the orphanage in India, but you can increase the chances you will recognize them—truly "see" these life-changing frames from the film roll of your routine—quickly and respond properly. It begins with daily surrender to God that transforms everyday life into an adventure of obedience.

If you are hungry for the heartlinks of passion, I encourage you to try beginning your day with this simple prayer. There is nothing special about the exact words, but you might find it helpful to copy this into your prayer journal or put it in your Bible until you make it your own.

*Father God, I surrender myself to You again today. I am Your servant, and You are my Master. I acknowledge all that I am and everything I have belongs to You. The longing of my heart, though well beyond my reach, is for every moment of this day to be a white-hot passionate pursuit of a straight path toward intimacy with You. I want my life to be centered, anchored, and rooted in You. I want everything I see, think, say, and do today to bring You glory, to be honoring and pleasing to You. If at any moment today my attention, my direction, or my focus turns even the slightest bit to the right or the left, please, Father, like the needle of a compass turns back to true north, turn my focus back toward You.*

*Father, I affirm that a central thread of my purpose in life is to join with You in blessing others, including those who are not like me, don't like me, won't thank me, and can't repay me. Make this day an adventure of obedience, and open my eyes to see what You see around me today. I am more concerned about missing an opportunity to bless others today than I am about looking foolish or being misunderstood or taken advantage of or putting myself at risk. I know life is not about preserving my comfort zone or eliminating danger. Lead me to the life-shaping experiences that will open the wellspring of passion in my life. Help me take the initiative today in crossing boundaries and overcoming barriers to show Your mercy by serving others. In Jesus' name, amen.*

# Chapter 5

# FOUR DOMAINS OF PASSIONATE ENGAGEMENT

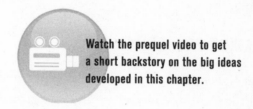

Watch the prequel video to get a short backstory on the big ideas developed in this chapter.

The greatest challenges of any moment in history cannot be adequately addressed by people who flutter from one cause to the next like bees in search of pollen on a hot summer day. People who jump on and off passion bandwagons like sports fans looking for the hottest team at playoff time could be better described as "fassionate" than passionate. They are naive idealists at best and "slacktivists" at worst, more concerned about making a name for themselves than making a difference in the lives of others.

Complex problems call for committed people. Chronic and epidemic challenges that generate sustained urgency, such as human trafficking, AIDS orphans, or the oppression of Dalits, will be resolved only by people who demonstrate high levels of issue-based passion over long periods of time. It is unreasonable to suggest only the individuals with physical proximity to these problems have the responsibility to deal with them. As we have discovered, God uses life-shaping experiences to establish heartlinks that enable us to organize and prioritize the most important answers to the question, "Who is my neighbor?"

As you begin to identify your issue-based passions, it will be important to recognize the need for focus over balance. You should not expect to give equal amounts of time, money, and creative energy to every issue that comes your way, but just because you can't do everything doesn't mean you can't do something. The value of allowing the God-ordained heartlinks established through life-shaping experiences to PageRank your passions comes by informing your decision to give priority to some needs over others. Passionate action will make you more like a river than a flood. Understanding this process is powerfully liberating; it plays a central role in overcoming the dangers of information overload and compassion fatigue. But it can also predispose us to another danger I describe as passion projection.

## PASSION PROJECTION

The higher you move up the passion pyramid, from learning to engaging to influencing, even when it calls for sacrificing time, money, and energy, the more tempting it will become to evaluate the level of passion in others using your own journey as a benchmark. We tend to view people who are not involved with our issue-based passions as uncommitted, and people who claim to share our passion but employ a different strategy for action as misguided. When the line between passion and strategy is blurred, we more readily assume others who engage with a specific problem differently don't really care, aren't really passionate.

The reality is that God gives different people heartlinks to different passions so everything He wants to do gets done. God leads people with a diversity of gifting to different strategies for engaging the same passion because He knows it will take a multifaceted approach to truly make a difference. Take the challenge of abortion, for example.

Most Christ followers would agree that abortion, which snuffs out a life when it is most vulnerable, is wrong. For many the pro-life cause has become an issue-based passion; they are self-motivated to learn more about it, engage in activities to stop it, influence others to join the cause, and pay a price for all of the above. But among those who are passionately pro-life, some believe the best strategy is to protest clinics and take non-violent emergency steps to stop the killing. Others, equally passionate, feel inclined to provide practical help to single moms and those with unplanned pregnancies who are most at risk to have an abortion. Some feel the best strategy is to work the political angle and do everything possible to change the law. Still others believe eliminating abortion altogether is ideal but unrealistic and want to help solve the problem by finding ways to reduce the number of abortions.

In reality, all of these strategies are important and should be pursued simultaneously, albeit with grace-awakened initiative, recognizing that without love our words and actions are as unwelcome as the creaking of a rusty gate (see 1 Corinthians 13:1, MSG). The different approaches are complimentary, not contradictory. Yet too often high levels of issue-based passion cause activists to devalue the contribution of others, especially when they approach the problem from a different direction.

## FOUR DOMAINS OF PASSIONATE ENGAGEMENT

My experience in coaching people toward a focused life, fueled by issue-based passions, has led me to believe there are four domains of passionate engagement:

- Service, focused on meeting a need
- Justice, focused on righting a wrong
- Discovery, focused on solving a problem
- And advocacy, focused on promoting a cause

The bigger and more complex the issue, the more likely it will require passionate engagement from all four domains to make a lasting impact. Devaluing the contribution of others who share your passion but are operating in a different domain is to have zeal without wisdom (see Proverbs 19:2). It is as foolish as the head telling the feet, "I don't need you" (1 Corinthians 12:21).

| | |
|---|---|
| **Service:** focused on meeting a need | **Justice:** focused on righting a wrong |
| **Discovery:** focused on solving a problem | **Advocacy:** focused on promoting a cause |

**Four Domains of Passionate Engagement**

These four domains of passionate engagement should not be viewed as rigid categories. But they can be helpful when seeking to find your own sweet spot for engagement and recognizing where you will need to be intentional about enlisting the help of others. There is no hard and fast formula that suggests certain combinations of temperament, strengths, or gifts will automatically place a person in one domain or another. And yet people with the strength of empathy as well as the gift of mercy or serving often gravitate toward the service domain with a bent toward meeting practical needs. Those with "word gifts" such as teaching or the strength to woo others may gravitate toward advocacy. People with a bent toward analytical thinking may find themselves repeatedly asking why, with a focus on solving a problem in the discovery domain. Still others will have strengths that point toward righting a wrong in the pursuit of justice.

It is common for people to feel drawn to more than one domain, but there is almost always a greater affinity for one over another. I was explaining the four domains to a friend over breakfast, and he listened with enthusiasm, affirming my categories while lamenting the fact that he was equally invested in all four. Yet he had just finished explaining a book project he was working on about sharing Jesus with others. It was clear based on what he had told me about the book that he was operating dominantly in the discovery domain with a focus on solving a problem. He was concerned about the fact that many Christ followers struggle to have natural conversations with others about Jesus. He had spent lots of time asking the why question and was passionate about solving this problem. On further reflection he agreed that at least for this particular passion he was operating dominantly in the discovery domain and secondarily in the advocacy domain.

## OBSERVATIONS ABOUT THE FOUR DOMAINS

Almost everyone begins to engage issue-based passions in the service domain with some attempt to meet a practical need. Amy Carmichael started out serving young girls in her neighborhood and later rescuing temple girls in India. While her ministry with the Dohnavur Fellowship continued to provide a place of refuge for temple girls, she eventually gravitated toward the justice domain, seeking to right a wrong by making the practice of selling a girl child to a Hindu temple illegal. You can expect to begin your journey toward action in the service domain, but don't be surprised if eventually you find yourself moving toward one of the other three domains.

People who begin in the justice, discovery, or advocacy domain will need some experience in the service domain in order to remain credible with others. Celebrity spokespersons who can't share anything meaningful from the grassroots domain of service will be left with borrowed stories that eventually leave the people they want to influence wondering about their depth of commitment. Similarly, people operating in the justice and discovery domain will need input from the service domain to ensure their work is pertinent and relevant.

Not every issue-based passion will call for activity in each domain, or at least the need for engagement in the justice and discovery domains may not be as obvious. Passions that are more associated with a means as opposed to an end can be one step removed from the justice and discovery domains. For example, one of my passions is leadership and leader development. But leadership is not an end in itself; it is a means to some other end. For me the end beyond the means of leadership is the Great Commission, Jesus' command to "go and make disciples of all nations" (Matthew 28:19). I'm passionate about developing leaders because I know you can't even start a new small group without a small group leader, not to mention planting a new church or engaging an unreached people group. When viewed in this light, leadership connected to the Great Commission, it is easier to understand how the four domains of passionate engagement come into play. For this reason I believe leadership is actually an interest-based rather than an issue-based passion. The same could be said about politics or business, coaching, or training, along with other issues that are more associated with a means or method instead of an end or cause. Interest-based passions are important and can interact powerfully with issue-based passions. We'll look at how in the next chapter.

Finally, the service domain on the top left of the diagram is more of a grassroots, bottom-up engagement that involves direct activities that make a difference. Advocacy, at the bottom right of the diagram, is more like a mountaintop engagement utilizing indirect activities. Almost everything in the service domain starts in the trenches and directly engages the problem at the grassroots level, whether it is feeding the homeless, removing trash from an open space, or showing God's love to prostitutes in a seedy part of town. Almost everything in the advocacy domain starts at the 20,000-foot level, raising awareness about the need and seeking to mobilize others to get involved. Both the discovery and justice domains can bend either way, toward bottom-up engagement at the grassroots or indirect engagement that is more top-down.

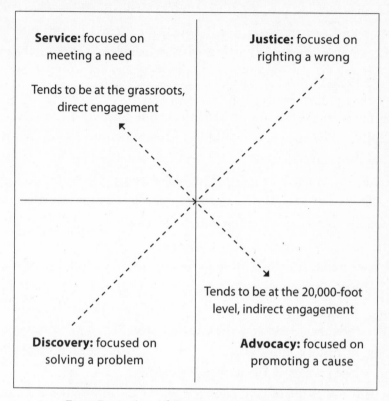

**Four Domains of Passionate Engagement**

---

By purchasing this book you receive a one-time FREE access to www.MyPassionProfile.com, developed by Steve Moore in partnership with Growing Leaders. MyPassionProfile.com is an online assessment designed to give you a model and a framework for (1) exploring areas of issue-based passion, (2) reality testing the level of passion you have for up to three issue-based passions, and (3) providing common language about passion that enables you to connect with an online community of like-minded and like-hearted people. For information on how to access your one-time free assessment, send an e-mail to neighbor@MyPassionProfile .com. You will receive an auto-responder message with all the information you need to get started.

---

I realize for most people passion is a lot like quality; it's hard to define, but we know it when we see it. My attempts to demystify this subject by identifying the two streams of interest- and issue-based passion, the pyramid of progression from learning to engaging to influencing and sacrificing, as well as the four domains of passionate engagement, can make the mysterious appear mechanical. But I believe these labels and principles can become keys that unlock the ability to see passion in yourself and the people around you. The more you understand how passion is forged in the crucible of life-shaping experiences, the better positioned you will be to PageRank your heartlinks and focus your initiative, crossing boundaries and overcoming barriers to show God's mercy by serving others.

I have found the breakthrough in applying these principles to one's own journey often comes by looking out the window as opposed to in the mirror. We are more inclined to see the principles of passion at work in the lives of others first and then in ourselves. Look with me out the window of history into the journey of one of the greatest examples of passion-fueled action in the service of others.

The life of William Wilberforce is one of the most powerful illustrations of level-four passion, demonstrating a commitment to learn more about, engage in, and influence others toward an issue, even when it called for personal sacrifice. Beginning in his twenties, Wilberforce continued to press forward for over two decades with his commitment to abolish the slave trade in the British Empire. Engaging this great cause was hardly a campaign strategy to get noticed in a crowded political field. Wilberforce could not be accused of being "fassionate" about the slave trade in an effort to leverage favorable winds of political fortune. Yet he was by no means the first person to arrive at this dance with destiny, and he did not undertake the journey alone. Even a casual review of the story confirms it would not have been successful without a team of partners operating in all four domains of passionate engagement.

## THE CHICKEN OR THE EGG?

In his biography on the life of Wilberforce, *Amazing Grace*, Eric Metaxas states, "The events that launched Wilberforce in his historical quest are as impossible to sort out as whether the proverbial chicken can be said to have laid the proverbial egg or to have been hatched from it."[1] There are some obvious heartlinks in Wilberforce's journey, not the least of which is his relationship with John Newton as a middle-school-aged child. Newton's autobiography, *An Authentic Narrative*, had been written a decade before and was still wildly popular; if Wilberforce had not read it himself, he certainly knew the story. It may have informed an essay he wrote at age fourteen, "in which he decried the business of slavery."[2]

Whatever the heartlinks in his childhood years, Wilberforce reflecting on his first year in Parliament said, "I had been strongly interested for the West Indian slaves, and I expressed my hope, that I should redress the wrongs of those wretched beings."[3] In his own words, William Wilberforce, at age twenty, describes a self-directed interest in the issue-based passion that would dominate his life and a preference for the justice domain, focused on righting a wrong. But in taking his place in the justice domain, he would be coming alongside, or perhaps standing on the shoulders of, Granville Sharp, who was his elder by twenty-four years.

## JUSTICE AS A GATEWAY TO PASSIONATE ENGAGEMENT

Granville Sharp was a contradiction of talent and eccentricity. He was a renowned musician living on a floating barge with most of his family, who formed a band that played primarily for people of privilege, including royals. He was well connected, with a brother who not only played in the family band but also served as the official surgeon to the king. In 1765, Granville Sharp encountered a young African slave on a street in London. The young man had been beaten within an inch of his life and discarded. No doubt hundreds of other people saw the severely wounded slave but passed by on the other side.

"Granville Sharp was one of those Christian fanatics who took the injunction to love one's neighbor literally—who loved neighbors even when they were inconvenient African neighbors trying to reclaim their freedom."[4] Just as Jesus had commanded, Sharp took the initiative to cross boundaries and overcome barriers to show God's mercy by serving others, even when they were not like him and couldn't repay him. Like the Good Samaritan, Sharp took the young slave, Jonathan Strong, to his brother's clinic on Mincing Lane, where he received emergency care. Once he was stabilized, they took him to a hospital and paid for his extended stay. Strong's injuries were so severe that it took four months in the hospital for him to recover.

As is often the case, this initial engagement with the slave trade came through the service domain, focused on meeting a need. But two years after Jonathan Strong had been rescued by the merciful initiative of the Sharp brothers, he was spotted by David Lisle, the lawyer and slave owner who had pistol-whipped him and tossed him out on the street like human rubbish. Lisle was amazed to discover his property was still alive and now quite valuable. He had Strong kidnapped and put in jail while he sought for a buyer. Word came to Granville Sharp, who again came to the rescue, leveraging his vast network and demonstrating a bulldoglike tenacity that convinced Lisle to release his claim. The incident engaged Sharp's curiosity and catapulted him into a study of English law. His self-taught legal expertise would place him at the center of another high-profile case regarding an African man named Somerset who, though a slave in Virginia, had been brought to London and was demanding his freedom. Building on several years of obsessive study, Granville pressed the case in the courts and won a narrow victory. The judge ruled that Somerset was free without applying the decision to the fourteen thousand other slaves in England. The celebration surrounding the case resounded throughout the abolition movement and beyond, triggering a growing choir of voices who joined Granville Sharp in decrying the evils of slavery. And the echoes of those voices could still be heard when William Wilberforce made his public entrance into the justice domain as an expression of passionate engagement for the same cause.

## ADVOCACY AS A GATEWAY TO PASSIONATE ENGAGEMENT

Thomas Clarkson entered the abolition movement through an unlikely set of circumstances. As a twenty-five-year-old divinity student at St. John's College, the same school Wilberforce had attended a few years earlier, he entered an annual Latin essay contest sponsored by Cambridge University. The vice chancellor, an Anglican minister named Peter Peckard, had a growing distaste for the slave trade and chose to focus the annual essay on the question, "Is it lawful to enslave others against their will?" This contest was especially prestigious, padding the award winner's résumé for life.

Clarkson was a devout Christ follower but had not given much thought at all to the slave trade. He was a motivated student who set his sights on winning the highly coveted essay contest with little thought about ending the slave trade. But as he threw himself into hours of rigorous study, the information Clarkson gleaned birthed a wellspring of compassion. The pressure of that wellspring of knowledge gathered steam like a geyser ready to burst forth from the soil of Clarkson's heart.

Thomas Clarkson's essay won the prize, but he was no longer satisfied with padding his résumé. He was feeling compelled toward action. After completing his studies, he left Cambridge for London on horseback. The information he had gathered for his essay haunted him to the point that he dismounted his horse near Herefordshire. "It was a moment he would remember for the rest of his long life. For it was there and then, on the side of the road, that it first occurred to Thomas Clarkson that if the things he had uncovered and written about in his prize-winning essay were a reality . . . it was time someone put an end to them."[5]

His first step was to translate his Latin essay into English and distribute it. He had become an unlikely advocate in the abolitionist cause. After publically declaring his decision to a full-time commitment to the cause of ending slavery, "he would from that point forward be unflagging in his efforts to stir up public zeal by distributing copies of his essay."[6] Effective advocacy requires solid information. Clarkson had done significant research for his essay, but the self-directed motivation to keep learning more about the horrors of slavery overtook Clarkson like a raging storm. It is said that before he was through Clarkson had interviewed as many as twenty thousand sailors.

Others would be invited to contribute their talents to the cause. John Newton was asked to persuade his friend William Cowper to write a poem. He submitted "The Negro's Complaint," which helped widen the circle of information. An artist named Josiah Wedgwood created an image of a kneeling slave, shackled both hand and foot, looking upward to ask, "Am I not a man and a brother?" This may have been the first logo ever created for a human rights campaign. It was printed on everything from snuff boxes to jewelry pinned by ladies to their dresses and in their hair. It was even made into a letter-sealing fob to imprint the wax used to seal letters.

Thomas Clarkson came into possession of a slave-ship schematic that showed in great detail how to position slaves to maximize their numbers as human cargo. To slave traders it was a stale expression of business-process optimization with a free market focus on the bottom line. To the growing number of people taking a fresh look at the slave trade, due in part to Clarkson and his network of advocates, it was a "nightmare of understatement."[7] Clarkson meticulously reworked the diagram using the measurements of a specific slave ship owned by one of the wealthiest families in Liverpool. At first glance the images could be anything from meaningless marks to antlike creatures. But upon closer examination the detailed drawing showed people; the smaller ones must be children. It was distributed everywhere, becoming as horrifying as it was ubiquitous.

The advocacy expression of passionate engagement had cobbled together an unlikely group of artists and poets whose diverse gifting helped build the groundswell of support that paved the way for Wilberforce. At five in the evening on May 12, 1789, Wilberforce would make the speech of his life, speaking extemporaneously before Parliament for three and a half hours. But in spite of his meticulous, logical, and powerful argument, the effort to pass anti–slave trade legislation fell short. Another approach would be needed, one driven by the curious desire to solve a problem.

# DISCOVERY AS A GATEWAY TO PASSIONATE ENGAGEMENT

The string of legislative defeats, beginning in 1789 and again in 1791, was more than Thomas Clarkson could bear. He eventually stepped away from active engagement in the cause for more than a decade. But as Clarkson exited the stage, another unlikely player arrived in London. His name was James Stephen. When Stephen was a child, his father had gone bankrupt, ending up in a debtor's prison. As strange as it seems today, incarcerated debtors were allowed to take their family with them. James Stephen spent some of his formative years in prison with his father.

As a young man exploring the nightlife in London, he found himself in a scandalous situation, engaged to two women at the same time, with one of them pregnant. He took the easy way out and fled the country, headed for the West Indies, where he would make a fortune. Upon arriving in Barbados in 1783, Stephen attended the trial of several African slaves who were widely believed to have been falsely accused. They were not only convicted but burned alive at the stake. The horrific sight formed a heartlink between James Stephen and the abolitionist cause.

Arriving in London, Stephen joined the network of abolitionists known as the Clapham Sect. His study of merchant law had led him to a discovery that would play a significant role in solving the problem Wilberforce had faced in fashioning legislation that would impact the slave trade and still be passed in Parliament.

The French were at war with England, and most slave ships conveniently sailed under the neutral American flag so as not to be liable to seizure by privately owned vessels commissioned by either the French or English government, to harass their enemy's sailing vessels. James Stephen proposed they introduce a bill that removed the protection of neutrality and authorized privateers to seize the cargo of French ships sailing under the American flag.

The movie *Amazing Grace* depicts Clarkson and Wilberforce interrupting Prime Minister William Pitt's game of golf to present this strategy. For the life of him, Pitt could not see why this bill was important enough to warrant a special visit and interrupt his golf or what it had to do with the slave trade. The stealth nature of the bill was its brilliance. Wilberforce explained: "Eighty percent of all slave ships are flying the neutral American flag to prevent them from being boarded by privateers. If we pass a law removing their protection no ship owner will dare allow his vessel to make the journey." The bill would apply equally to both French and English ships since they both employed the same neutral flag strategy.

Wilberforce explained to Pitt that while the bill wouldn't put an end to the slave trade, it would cut their profits so deeply that as many as half of the traders would be bankrupt in two years. James Stephen had discovered a plan that was openly anti-French and secretly anti-slave. All that was needed was a boring parliamentarian with a reputation for patriotism to put the bill forward so as to protect the real motives behind it. The bill passed and turned the momentum back in Wilberforce's favor.

## SERVICE AS A GATEWAY TO PASSIONATE ENGAGEMENT

One of the by-products of the Somerset case that Granville Sharp had successfully argued was the increasing number of "negro beggars" on the streets of London. Also, many American slaves had been given freedom by joining the British forces during the war with the colonies. The work to abolish the slave trade continued, but the importance of meeting the needs of freed slaves became increasingly obvious.

In 1786 a Committee for Relieving the Black Poor was established; a key player in the formation of the committee was Dr. Smeathman, who had lived on the west coast of Africa and suggested a colony be formed there for freed slaves. The goal was to prove blacks were every bit as capable of governing themselves as the people who had enslaved them. It was hoped a thriving economy could be established to help form a beachhead of freedom. May 10, 1787, several hundred blacks arrived in Sierra Leone as the firstfruits of this well-intended experiment. But across the ocean in the West Indies, other Christ followers motivated by service to God and others had already been at work for more than three decades.

"The Moravians were extraordinary Christians who . . . ignored the high-toned sneering of the theologically compromised Church of England religious leaders, and quietly did what their faith in God called them to do."[8] They were committed to obedience, even when it required sacrifice. The leader of the Moravian movement was Count Zinzendorf, who while traveling in Denmark met a West Indian slave named Antony Ulrich. He told Zinzendorf as much about the spiritual need of his brethren as the evils of slavery. "If only some missionaries would come," said Ulrich, "they would certainly be heartily welcomed. Many an evening have I sat on the shore and sighed my soul toward Christian Europe; and I have a brother and sister in bondage who long to know the living God."[9]

Upon returning to the community he had founded in Herrnhut, Moravia, Zinzendorf shared his passion for missionary service among the slaves of the West Indies. Antony Ulrich came and addressed the congregation, explaining that no one could be a missionary in St. Thomas without first becoming a slave. In fact, Ulrich was innocently mistaken, but the young men who stepped forward to serve did so with the belief they were sacrificing their freedom for the privilege of crossing boundaries and overcoming barriers to show God's mercy by serving others.

Leonard Dober and David Nitschmann accepted this call and saw the firstfruits of Moravian missionary service. For fifty years the Moravian Brethren labored in the West Indies without aid from any other religious denomination. They established churches in St. Thomas, in St. Croix, in St. John's, in Jamaica, in Antigua, in Barbados, and in St. Kitts. They had thirteen thousand baptized converts before a missionary from any other church arrived on the scene.[10]

This epic struggle against the evil of the slave trade did not end in Wilberforce's day. The great strides made by the network of collaborators operating in each of the four domains of passionate engagement helped change the mind-set that had made slavery acceptable and allowed it to survive unchallenged for millennia. But the evils of bonded labor, human trafficking, the oppression of Dalits, and other forms of slavery still exist today. Efforts to chip away at their foundations will require a multifaceted approach that includes service, justice, discovery, and advocacy. It will require a diversity of people with varied gifting who are unified by a commitment to learn more about, engage in, and influence others toward noble, issue-based causes even when sacrifice is required. And it will call forth point leaders like Wilberforce who allow the raw fuel of passion to become a life of purpose.

Examples of passion-fueled purpose can be inspiring and overwhelming at the same time. A common danger is the temptation to evaluate the worth of one's purpose based on how it compares to others. This is one of the Devil's favorite traps. Some of us are tempted to compare our journey with individuals who we believe are less important and to think more highly of ourselves than we ought. Others are tempted to compare themselves with people whose lives are playing out on a "grander stage" and shrink back. These are like ditches on either side of the road, and the Enemy doesn't really care which one we land in as long as he can get us off track. Remember, it is not the scale of your purpose that matters but the Source.

Chapter 6

# PASSION-FUELED PURPOSE

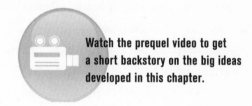

Watch the prequel video to get
a short backstory on the big ideas
developed in this chapter.

A great purpose is cumulative, and, like a great magnet, it attracts all that is kindred along the stream of life.[1] Wilberforce was a great magnet, and the network of collaborators that was drawn to him made all the difference. It was not the strength of his personality that attracted them but the greatness of his purpose. Long before the public victories in his enduring struggle to end the slave trade, Wilberforce had privately surrendered himself to God's purpose for his life, writing in his journal on October 28, 1787, "God almighty has set before me two great objects: the suppression of the slave trade and the reformation of manners."[2]

By the reformation of manners, Wilberforce was referring to a transformation in the habits and attitudes of the day with a distinctly moral overtone. He wanted to make "goodness fashionable." In spite of the fact that he was an up-and-coming politician, having been elected to Parliament seven years earlier at age twenty-one, Wilberforce's life purpose as defined by the two great objects appears ambitious at best and presumptuous at worst. Yet fueled by increasing levels of issue-based passion, William Wilberforce poured out his life like a drink offering in the pursuit of a God-honoring life purpose. His legacy stands as a powerful reminder of the admonition given by the apostle Paul: "Let us not become weary in doing good, for at the proper time we will reap a harvest if we do not give up" (Galatians 6:9).

As we have seen in the life of Amy Carmichael, C. T. Studd, and

William Wilberforce and his network of abolitionist leaders, God uses life-shaping experiences to establish heartlinks with issue-based passions. These heartlinks, like hyperlinks in Google's PageRank algorithm, help organize and prioritize the passions that fuel a life of purpose. While this process is not new, it is increasingly important today if we are to respond intelligently to the daily barrage of needs a Google-powered and connected world puts in the palms of our hands in real time. PageRanking your passions will help inform decisions about the causes toward which you leverage your time, gifts, and resources in the service of others. But answering the question, "Who is my neighbor?" and finding your way as a Good Samaritan in a connected world will require you to move beyond high levels of issue-based passion toward growing clarity about your life purpose.

## LIFE PURPOSE: THE TRIPLE BOTTOM LINE

Understanding your issue-based passions opens the door to the highest purpose for your life, connecting your deepest sense of fulfillment with your greatest sense of accomplishment. How can you know if you're pursuing the highest purpose for your life? It must bring glory to God and serve or add value to others. To reprise a supporting idea from the story of the Good Samaritan, it must be a God-first and others-focused agenda. But it will also connect your deepest sense of fulfillment with your greatest sense of accomplishment. When pursuing your highest purpose, you will never find yourself at the top of the ladder of success only to discover it is leaning against the wrong wall.

For Christ followers this kind of focused living pays a triple bottom line. When you pursue your life purpose, God receives the greatest glory, you receive the greatest joy, and the kingdom is most strategically advanced on the earth. There is nothing you could do in the time you are granted on earth that will bring God more glory than to fulfill His purpose for your life. In your wildest, most imaginative and creative moment, there is nothing you could envision doing with your life that would bring you more joy and fulfillment than what God has already designed. Regardless of how diligently and persistently you leverage your giftedness, no contribution will be more strategic than simply doing the "good works" God has already prepared in advance for you to do (Ephesians 2:10).

In pursuing your purpose, you will experience great joy, but it will not be easy. Life purpose is never the path of least resistance, which is why the renewable fuel of issue-based passion is so important. You will need the self-directed commitment to keep learning, engaging, and influencing, even when sacrifice is required.

## DISCOVERING YOUR LIFE PURPOSE: THE THREE VARIABLES

I have enough experience sharing about this topic to know that you may be tempted at this point to exempt yourself from this entire conversation, believing you are the exception to the rule. I want to make several brief and yet important assertions that I can state with great confidence. God has a purpose for everyone, including you. It is possible to discover your life purpose. God knows you can't do what He put you on the earth to do if you don't know what it is. Your purpose will be fueled by the God-honoring passions that emerge from the life-shaping experiences, the heartlinks that come your way. Pursuing your life purpose will bring freedom and clarity to the decisions you make about crossing boundaries and overcoming barriers to show God's mercy by serving others.

There is no simple formula for discovering your life purpose; it would be foolish to suggest you can plug information into a life-purpose spreadsheet, hit enter, and come away with an answer. But there are guideposts that can prove helpful. In my experience training and coaching people of all ages and diverse vocations in life planning, three variables have consistently shed light on the journey: history, identity, and opportunity. The history variable asks, "What are the clues from my journey so far?" The identity variable asks, "Who did God make me to be? What do I have to offer?" The opportunity variable asks, "How can I serve or add value to others?" Let's take a brief but closer look at each of these three variables.

## THE HISTORY VARIABLE

It has been said that the two most important moments in your life are when you were born and when you discovered why you were born. Discovering why you were born shines a light on your future but requires a look at your past. God has already been at work in your life. He wants to conform you to His image and prepare you to accomplish His purpose for your life. Though you may not have recognized these life-shaping, destiny-marker experiences when they occurred, if you stop and reflect on your journey so far, I believe you will find them. The idea of looking back to where you have come from for clues about where you are going seems counterintuitive. But in more ways than you might think, your past has helped shape who you are, and thereby influences what you do. Your history has a lot to do with your destiny.

You may find it helpful to reflect on your journey using several lenses or vantage points. Start by looking for formative relationships, asking the question, "What relationships have most significantly imprinted my life or shaped my journey?" Be on the lookout for unique friendships, mentors, or special circumstances in your family history. In the Bible, the stories of Joseph, Moses, Samson, and David, just to name a few, are sprinkled with examples of how God used life-shaping, destiny-marker experiences to lay the foundation for a special purpose.

A second lens for helpful reflection is personal milestones, using the question, "What significant events, experiences, or accomplishments have served as building blocks for my journey?" Pay special attention to experiences in which your giftedness began to surface, in which you were shown unusual favor from God or the encouragement and affirmation of others.

A third lens through which you can look at your history is pivotal turning points, using the question, "Have I experienced special windows of opportunity or made definitive choices that opened new doors or expanded my horizons?" Look for opportunities in which you were stretched beyond your comfort zone. Be sure to include failure experiences, especially when they became teachable moments that accelerated your learning.

A fourth lens for exploring your journey so far is recurring mega-themes, using the question, "Can I see an overarching theme or storyline that weaves together the threads of several life-shaping experiences into a single fabric?" For example, this could be an accelerated interest or even prodigy-like focus combined with recurring opportunities. It may be repeated encounters with different people who have similar needs.

Finally, consider reflecting on your history variable with the lens of providential occurrences, using the question, "Have I had 'unexplainable coincidences' or spiritual experiences that have shaped my life and marked my journey?" Be alert for God's providential intervention that spared your life, unusual circumstances surrounding your birth, or special guidance from God in decision making.

|  | **Primary Question** | **Possible Destiny Markers** |
|---|---|---|
| **Formative Relationships** | Q: What relationships have most significantly imprinted your life or shaped your journey? | • unique friendships<br>• mentor sponsors<br>• special heritage<br>• parental oath or commitment |
| **Personal Milestones** | Q: What significant events, experiences, or accomplishments have served as building blocks for your journey? | • giftedness discovery<br>• meaningful award or recognition<br>• special affirmation or encouragement |
| **Pivotal Turning Points** | Q: Have you experienced special windows of opportunity or made definitive choices that opened new doors or expanded your horizons? | • failing forward experiences<br>• expanded influence challenges<br>• life-shaping experiences |
| **Recurring Megathemes** | Q: Can you see an overarching thematic focal point toward which your life should be directed? | • accelerated interest<br>• prodigy-like focus<br>• recurring opportunities |
| **Providental Occurrences** | Q: Have you had "unexplainable coincidences" or overtly spiritual experiences that shaped your life or informed your journey? | • name significance<br>• unusual birth circumstances<br>• preservation of life experiences<br>• spiritually based guidance or revelation |

Before you discount this as too complex or mysterious, let me remind you of Amy Carmichael's journey from chapter 4. Amy's encounter with the little girl outside the tea shop was a powerful, life-shaping spiritual experience. The same could be said of her ministry to the "bag lady" during which she heard the voice of God, refining her motives. Amy's ministry to the young girls in her neighborhood and "shawlies" stimulated the discovery of her giftedness and refined her passion for the marginalized and neglected. The gift from Kate Mitchell that provided the funds for building the Welcome Hall demonstrated God's favor, expanding her influence and broadening her opportunities for ministry. All of this would converge as a megatheme in her life when she encountered the temple girl in India more than a decade later.

It is important that you understand these destiny markers seem so obvious in Amy's story only when years are compacted into a few sentences like time-lapse photography and the mundane routines of daily life are pruned from the narrative like overgrown branches on a vine. If you are in your twenties or younger, it is quite likely the most important life-shaping experiences that will heartlink you to issue-based passions and fuel your life purpose are still around the corner. Don't try to manufacture them. Remember the importance of daily surrender that can turn life into an ongoing adventure. Revisit the sample prayer at the close of chapter 4 that I pray almost every day, and expect God to lead you. Take time to reflect on your journey periodically using the lens of the history variable with a special priority for the issue-based passions that will provide the self-directed motivation required to fuel a life of great purpose.

One final thought before we move on. An unintended consequence of engaging the history variable can be running headlong into negative, even painful experiences in your past that you have tried very hard to forget. In some cases these trying or even tragic events raise profound questions such as "Where was God when this happened?" As difficult as it might be to accept, God is big enough to reach down into those painful moments with healing grace to set you free. He may even take the emotional wreckage of those experiences and build a platform for influence that will enable you to serve others who have been similarly wounded.

The tragic reality is that some people miss out on God's purpose for their lives not because they don't know what it is or believe it is good but because they are dragging around a ball and chain of hurt, anger, and resentment from their past. Joseph could easily have found himself in this kind of emotional and spiritual prison after having been sold by his brothers into slavery in Egypt. The injustice he experienced there added insult to injury. But by God's grace he was able to move forward, even recognizing that while his brothers meant to bring him harm, God turned it into something good (see Genesis 50:19-20). He stands ready to do that for you as well.

## THE IDENTITY VARIABLE

Passion doesn't reveal anything about capacity. Passion helps clarify the "what" of your life purpose, but in order to pursue your passions and accomplish your purpose, you will need to know "how" in addition to "what." The question of "how" focuses attention on who God made you to be and what you have to offer in the service of others.

After all, the same God who designed a purpose for your life put the gifts and skills and tools inside you that would be needed to accomplish it. It is true that no matter how fully you develop your giftedness, you will need God's help and the help of others to accomplish your life purpose. But you cannot expect God to reward your failure to identify, develop, and steward all that He has entrusted to you by pouring out an extra measure of supernatural grace. In the same way that your history has a lot to do with your destiny, who God made you to be helps reveal what He wants you to do.

Engaging the identity variable is simply being honest with yourself about yourself, and honest about yourself with others. It is important that you grow in your self-awareness as it relates to your personality and temperament, your strengths, your acquired skills, and your spiritual gifts, in addition to your passions. There are many different assessment tools that can help you in this journey. Understanding who God made you to be will provide strategic information regarding the development of personal growth goals. I have written extensively on the importance of personal growth planning and how it relates to the pursuit of your life purpose in *The Dream Cycle: Leveraging the Power of Personal Growth*.

The reason God gave you the personality, strengths, skills, and gifts you have is that He knew you would need them to pursue the dominant issue-based passions that fuel your life purpose. But all of the strengths and gifts you received from God came in seed form. If you have the gift of serving or teaching or leadership, it did not come fully developed. God is expecting you to intentionally work those giftedness muscles to strengthen your ability to leverage those kingdom resources in the service of others. Regardless of which of the four domains of passionate engagement toward which you gravitate (service, justice, discovery, or advocacy), you will need to refine and develop your capacity to make the contribution God wants you to make.

## The Opportunity Variable

When it comes to your life purpose, the most strategic opportunities to serve others will come at the intersection of "what" and "how." By *what*, I mean your highest priority issue-based passions, and by *how*, I mean the gifts, skills, and tools God has put inside you. But a central theme of this book is that in a connected, globalized world, we live in virtual proximity to more needs than any one of us could possibly meet. Not every need will overlap with your passions and life purpose. God has prepared good works in advance for you to do, but clearly that divinely ordered project list is limited in scope. It is understandable and appropriate for you to use the passions that fuel your life purpose to filter the opportunities that come your way.

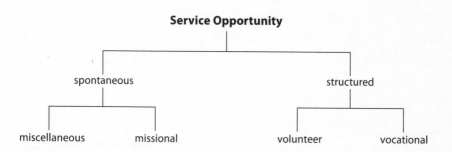

Opportunities to use your giftedness in areas that connect with your life purpose will generally fit in one of two categories: structured or spontaneous. Spontaneous opportunities to serve others are usually momentary, unplanned, and one-off situations that can further be divided into miscellaneous and missional. By *miscellaneous* I mean opportunities that do not overlap with the sweet spot of your purpose and capacity, but the combination of proximity and urgency suggest action is appropriate. To revisit the tragic story of Eutisha Rennix in the opening chapter of this book, if you came across a twenty-five-year-old pregnant woman who had passed out, you would probably feel responsible to do something to help while you waited for first responders to arrive, even if you were not a trained EMT.

I am not mechanically inclined at all and wouldn't have the faintest idea how to help a stranded motorist. I have enough self-awareness to recognize the aptitude and acquired skills required are beyond my capacity. I will never be involved in a ministry to help single mothers get their cars repaired or oil changed. That might fit in the sweet spot of someone else's issue-based passions and the good works God has prepared for them, but not mine. In spite of all this, if I came across a young mother and her van-load of kids stranded on the side of the road in apparent distress, I would view it as a spontaneous, albeit miscellaneous, opportunity to serve. I would stop, knowing full well my capacity to help begins and ends with my cell phone.

In addition to spontaneous/miscellaneous, there are also spontaneous/missional opportunities to serve others. These are unplanned and often momentary encounters where God places someone in your path whose need overlaps with both your passions and giftedness. I believe this happens much more often than you think, but if you have not refined your understanding of your passions, purpose, and the kingdom resources you are vested with, you will not see them.

There is a simple but powerful principle that says what you focus on expands. For example, several years ago my wife and I purchased a Honda Odyssey, after years of driving another brand. Almost immediately after purchasing our new van, I started seeing other Honda Odysseys everywhere. Did our purchasing decision start an immediate trend? No. The fact is there were already thousands of Honda Odysseys on the road, but I had never paid any attention to them. Once I started focusing on this specific model, I could hardly go around the block without noticing one. What you focus on expands.

The same will be true with the issue-based passions that fuel your life purpose. As you might expect based on the content of this book, one of my issue-based passions is helping people discover and live out their God-ordained purpose. I often have the opportunity to travel as an extension of my role as the president and CEO of The Mission Exchange. I routinely pray as I'm preparing for a trip, asking God to direct me to people who are hungry for greater meaning and purpose in their lives. I expect when I get where I'm going, as well as along the way, there will be a handful of divinely appointed conversations with people who are at a major crossroads in their lives. I believe the life experiences and kingdom resources God has deposited in me could be of help. Engaging them with thoughtful questions and Spirit-led prayer is part of the good works God has prepared in advance for me. Meeting people like this, even once for a few minutes, represents a spontaneous and yet missional opportunity to serve.

Even more important than spontaneous opportunities to serve others, you need to be aware of structured environments, including volunteer and vocational. As you might expect, structured opportunities for service are planned, recurring, and systematic points of engagement. Spontaneous windows of opportunity choose you. You choose the structured pathways of service and therefore should give special priority to ensuring they fit well with your giftedness and overlap as much as possible with your passions. These are the places where you will move toward level four on the passion pyramid, sacrificing as needed to learn more about, engage with, and influence others toward a worthy cause.

There are both volunteer and vocational expressions of structured service. You have probably heard motivational speakers exhort people not to waste another minute doing something they don't love to do. They tell you to find something you are passionate about that people will pay you to do. In a perfect world I agree. Robert Frost put it like this: "My object in living is to unite my avocation and vocation as my two eyes make one in sight."[3] But I am convinced that the overwhelming majority of "good works" God has prepared in advance for each of us will happen outside the walls of vocational service, even for professional ministers or Christian workers.

In chapter 4 I introduced you to two streams of passion, interest- and issue-based. At the confluence of these two streams is what I describe as "incarnational passion." Remember, interest-based passions are activities we pursue for fun; they bring us pleasure. Issue-based passions bring fulfillment and give a sense of purpose. Incarnational passions bring these two streams together, allowing us to combine the momentum of doing something we like to do for a cause we care deeply about.

For example, Nancy G. Brinker found an incarnational passion after her sister, Susan G. Koman, died of breast cancer. Having promised her dying sister she would work to spare other women from suffering in the same way, Nancy needed a tool to raise awareness and funds. While engaging an interest-based passion of jogging, she developed the initial idea of 5K races that have become known as Race for the Cure, which has helped fund more than $180 million in research grants for this issue-based cause.

## TURNING THE LENS—INCREASING FOCUS

If you would like additional information on the subject of life purpose, consider downloading the Life Planning webinar by Steve Moore from the online store at www.TheMissionExchange.org. Use the one-time discount code chapter6-neighbor to download this webinar for free.

It is helpful to view the model I have developed for discovering your life purpose as a lens that you turn by engaging the history, identity, and opportunity variables. Doing so brings your life purpose into focus. It enables your issue-based passions to fuel the highest purpose for your life, connecting your deepest sense of fulfillment with your greatest sense of accomplishment. This is not a linear, formulaic process. It is common for people to have more fully engaged the identity variable, growing in self-awareness as it relates to their giftedness, before ever seriously reflecting on their history variable. I'm not really concerned about whether you agree with my model, labels, or definitions. What I do care about is helping you identify the "great objects" God Almighty has set before you so you can begin to prioritize and organize your service of others around the highest purpose for your life. In doing so not only will you be following in the steps of William Wilberforce, but you will be doing what Jesus did.

## JESUS ON PURPOSE

If there was ever an acid test of the biblical validity of knowing and fulfilling your life purpose, it would be seeing this principle played out in the life of Jesus. Did Jesus have issue-based passions? Did He know His destiny and actively work together with God to fulfill it? Did He wander through life engaging in random acts of kindness until He ended up on a cross?

The answer to these questions depends to a certain extent on your Christology—your theology about Jesus. I believe that Jesus was all God and all man. He never stopped being God while on the earth, and yet He chose to put off the fullness of His divine nature so He could completely identify with our humanity. Jesus did miracles and worked wonders not because He was God but because as the God-man he drew upon the power of the Father through the Holy Spirit. He testified to this, saying, "I tell you the truth, the Son can do nothing by himself; he can do only what he sees his Father doing, because whatever the Father does the Son also does" (John 5:19).

It is this putting off of the divine nature that makes Jesus' identification with us so powerful. "For we do not have a high priest who is unable to sympathize with our weaknesses, but we have one who has been tempted in every way, just as we are—yet was without sin" (Hebrews 4:15). If it was not possible for Jesus to sin, but He merely exposed Himself to tempting situations to make us feel better, the incarnation is a cruel hoax.

In as much as Jesus chose not to sin, He chose to embrace the life purpose that had been ordained for Him from the foundation of the world. The first words of Jesus recorded in the Bible remind us that He had to be about His Father's business (see Luke 2:49). And from the earliest moments of His public ministry, He went out of His way to prove it. Jesus launched His public ministry in Nazareth, where on the Sabbath

He took His turn to read from the Scriptures. He stood up and unrolled the scroll of Isaiah, looking for a specific text. Upon finding it, Jesus read, "'The Spirit of the Lord is on me, because he has anointed me to preach good news to the poor. He has sent me to proclaim freedom for the prisoners and recovery of sight for the blind, to release the oppressed, to proclaim the year of the Lord's favor.' Then he rolled up the scroll, gave it back to the attendant and sat down. The eyes of everyone in the synagogue were fastened on him, and he began by saying to them, 'Today this scripture is fulfilled in your hearing'" (Luke 4:17-21). Jesus knew who He was and where He was going. He had discovered His destiny and declared it publicly.

After this incident at the synagogue in Nazareth, Jesus was literally run out of town. He moved from there to Capernaum, and on the Sabbath began to teach in the synagogue. Peter owned a home in this city, and Jesus had already developed a relationship with him through his brother Andrew. The people of Capernaum were receptive to Jesus' ministry, and many were healed or delivered from demons. This had the makings of an extensive base for Jesus. He was popular, people were responsive, and Peter's home provided a place to stay. At least that's what we might expect.

But Jesus spent some quality time alone with the Father one morning. The people of Capernaum came looking for Him. They urged Him to capitalize on the momentum of receptivity and opportunity. It made absolutely no sense for Jesus to leave Capernaum. But He did, saying, "I must preach the good news of the kingdom of God to the other towns also, *because that is why I was sent*" (Luke 4:43). Jesus repeatedly yielded to the Father's direction, filtering decisions based on His life purpose until eventually He could say, "I have brought you glory on earth by completing the work you gave me to do" (John 17:4).

The life example of Jesus reminds us it is possible to know your life purpose, use it as a filter for saying no to some opportunities and yes to others, and to press forward in obedience until that purpose is completed. A similar epitaph is given to David, who having "served God's purpose in his own generation . . . fell asleep" (Acts 13:36).

## WHERE'S THE SILVER BULLET?

Perhaps at this point in the book you are wondering, "Where's the silver bullet?" You may have been expecting me to pull a rabbit out of my hat and offer you a magical shortcut that will help you answer the once simple but increasingly complicated question, "Who is my neighbor?" I never promised anything of the sort. But I think I understand why you have this expectation. And I want to address it head on with a simple illustration.

Being a good steward of one's time has always been important. God didn't interrupt the flow of history one day with a new declaration saying, "Okay, now that you have learned how to write and invented the wheel, it appears life is getting a little too complicated and fast-paced. So I've determined that from now on, you have to be a good steward of your time, you have to redeem the days I have given you and use them wisely. Starting today." From Adam and Eve in the garden all the way to the end of time, God expects us to use every day wisely. He always has.

Similarly, the basic principles of organization and time management apply across the generations. Questions such as "What is most important? When does this need to be completed? Should I be doing this at all?" have timeless value. But as life has become more complicated and the number of distractions as well as potential interruptions increased exponentially, it is more difficult and more important than ever to employ the principles of personal organization in order to steward our days wisely. Post-it notes with cryptic messages randomly placed like a yellow brick road from the bathroom mirror to the refrigerator door to the dashboard on the car to the edges of your computer monitor will not enable you to effectively manage the complexities of life in a connected world. But you already knew that.

The tools available for you to get organized have evolved from a technology standpoint just like the nature of the interruptions. But the underlying questions that will make the tools effective are much the same. What I am purporting in this book is that while people have always been surrounded by the needs of others, we are more likely to know about those needs in almost real time than ever before, regardless of whether they are across the street or the ocean. Proximity is no longer a limiting factor in our assessment of how much responsibility we should assume for the needs of others, especially when the needs are chronic as well as pandemic.

Throughout history, the people who have had the greatest impact on the world have been those who embarked on a God-honoring journey of passion-fueled purpose. Their passions surfaced through life-shaping experiences that heartlinked them to causes they cared deeply about. Information stimulated compassionate action as they crossed boundaries and overcame barriers to show God's mercy by serving others. Nothing about this is new, as I've demonstrated from the lives of people such as Amy Carmichael and William Wilberforce. But just as managing your schedule is more complicated today than ever, discerning which issue-based passions, which "wounded traveler" on the side of the road, you should give priority to in this shrinking global village is also more difficult.

If you choose the life-planning equivalent of randomly placed Post-it notes to sort out your answer to the question, "Who is my neighbor?" you are almost certain to be overwhelmed in a tsunami of human need. You will be tempted to retreat into an enclave of self-absorption, drowning out information about the needs of others with the triviality of status updates and the superficiality of pop culture. You will find it easier to opt for the exit ramps between compassion and action I referenced in chapter 3, until eventually "passing by on the other side" becomes a shortcut to the well-rehearsed excuses that justify inaction.

The solution I'm offering, that of surrender as a gateway to adventure, of allowing God to apply a spiritual algorithm that PageRanks your passions, using them to fuel a life of great purpose and filter your engagement as a Good Samaritan, is not new. It has always been important; in fact it has never been more essential.

## PAGERANKING THE PASSIONS OF JESUS

One of the philosophical and theological questions that almost every Christ follower asks at one time or another is why Jesus didn't heal every sick person, feed every hungry person, and liberate every captive He encountered. We could answer that by revisiting the assertion Jesus made, saying He could do nothing by Himself and only did what He saw His Father doing (see John 5:19). But that only raises another similar question: Why didn't the Father instruct Jesus to meet all these needs? We are left with the explanation Jesus gave the people in Capernaum: That is not why He was sent (see Luke 4:43). Clearly Jesus was willing to say no, to embrace the boundaries of the life purpose the Father had given Him.

In part 3 of this book I want to explore a related question about the ministry and mission of Jesus. What issues or causes would be PageRanked to the top of the metaphorical search list for Jesus, organizing and prioritizing the universal passions of the kingdom? Can we identify issue-based passions that have been selectively emphasized in the Bible and resonate with the life purpose Jesus announced to the worshippers at the synagogue in Nazareth? I believe we can. And though you might not feel my list is complete, I don't think you will question if it is accurate. Keep in mind I'm not suggesting this is all God cares about. I am asserting that three issue-based passions rise to the top of the PageRank: the poor, the oppressed, and the lost. In addition to the unique passions that flow from your heartlinked life-shaping experiences, the more you become like Jesus, the more these three universal passions of the kingdom will be reflected in your journey.

# Part 3

# CONNECTING WITH GOD'S PASSIONS

# Chapter 7

# GOD'S PASSION FOR THE ULTRAPOOR

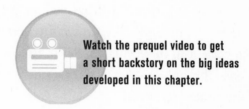

Watch the prequel video to get a short backstory on the big ideas developed in this chapter.

Everyone has the same need for food, but not everyone has the same access to provision. I'm using the word *food* as a metaphor for life's basic needs, which of course extends beyond something to eat every day to water and shelter at a minimum. It is interesting to note when those of us who live in relative affluence define the basic needs of people in the developing world, we make a pretty short list. If making a similar list for ourselves, it would likely include cable television and a cell phone. It's all about perspective. Everyone has the same need for food; not everyone has the same access to provision.

One of the formative experiences that confronted me with the complexity of poverty took place in a rural village in south India. I was talking with my Indian friend Samuel Stephens, president of India Gospel League, when we were approached by a man carrying a young girl. At first glance I thought this little girl had fallen asleep on her father's shoulder. But as he came closer I realized she was awake but too weak to even lift her head. A growth the size of an orange had disfigured one side of her face.

The man spoke softly to Sam, who with compassion in his voice asked several questions as he sought to piece together their story. I positioned myself so I could see the little girl's face and looked into her eyes. She was listless; disfigured and beautiful all at the same time. Sam spoke to the man in Tamil, so my mind was free to wander. Eerily I found myself picturing my youngest daughter's face on this little girl's body; they appeared very close in age. I could sense the helplessness in this man's voice. I couldn't understand his words, but I could relate with his father's heart.

The conversation lasted only a few minutes before Sam invited me to join him in praying over the little girl. We cried out to God, asking for His healing power to be displayed in her body. Divine intervention through healing and deliverance often creates beachheads of kingdom advancement in these villages, but in this instance there was no immediate breakthrough. As they walked away, the little girl's head never moved off her father's shoulder.

Once they left I raised the question I had been dying to ask: "Why did he wait so long to seek help?" I was more naive than judgmental. Sam explained that this family lived in a remote, rural setting where no medical care of any kind was available. India Gospel League brought mobile clinics to the region from time to time, which prompted the father to seek us out after hearing a team was in the area. Unfortunately, our group did not have a medical component. But this father's dilemma went well beyond the lack of access to medical treatment. Sam explained to me that he had traveled on foot for nearly half a day to speak to us. It would take the rest of the day to get home. That meant he would have no income for the day. But complicating things even more, since money earned from working every day is used to buy food for their only meal, his family would have to go without that night.

Taking his daughter to a clinic or hospital in a more urban environment would mean an even more complicated and expensive journey. Since they had no savings to fall back on, his family would have to forgo eating for several days to pull together the money needed for the trip. When including round-trip travel time on foot and bus, he would be leaving the rest of his family without food for the better part of a week. All this would need to be balanced with the unlikely hope that he would find a place willing and able to treat his daughter.

As I tried to get my mind around the emotional angst associated with a decision such as that, Sam looked at me and said, "His situation is not unique; there are thousands more just like him." I wasn't outside a tea shop in Belfast, but the compassion of God was aroused in my heart. I didn't write it in my journal that night, but like Amy Carmichael, in a moment of honest reflection, I had to admit, "As of now, I do nothing for little girls like you." Fifteen years later, I can still see that little girl's face. Our family has been sponsoring children with India Gospel League ever since.

Sam explained to me later that night that he had given this man money to cover the basic expenses he would incur to get to a hospital run by India Gospel League. Unsure of her prognosis, I knew his daughter would receive quality care by people who love Jesus, but I couldn't help but wonder about the millions of others just like him in India and beyond. Everyone has the same need for food; not everyone has access to provision.

## THE GOD OF THE POOR

It is not hard to make a case for the fact that the Holy Spirit guided the authors of the Bible to selectively emphasize the needs of the poor. It is said there are more than two thousand verses in the Bible on the subject of poverty.[1] One of the most quoted verses on this subject has repeatedly been used to justify a lack of compassionate action because only the first part of the verse is cited: "There will always be poor people in the land" (Deuteronomy 15:11). But the rest of the verse gives God's clear directive: "Therefore I command you to be openhanded toward your brothers and toward the poor and needy in your land." We are tempted to look at the first part of this verse and assume that since poverty will never be eradicated, there is justifiable reason for inaction. When the entire verse is viewed in context, it is clear that poverty provides a perpetual opportunity for Good Samaritan activity. Once again, it's all about perspective.

Jesus placed the poor at the epicenter of His life-purpose statement. Reading from the scroll of Isaiah in the synagogue in Nazareth, Jesus said He came to "preach good news to the poor" (Luke 4:18). Rich Stearns, in his book *The Hole in Our Gospel*, describes this passage in Luke as "the culmination and fulfillment of more than twenty centuries of God speaking to the nation of Israel through Moses and the prophets."[2] Jesus was not introducing a new idea.

Ministry to the poor remained central for the early church. The apostle Paul, describing words of encouragement and instruction about his ministry to the Gentiles, given to him by James, Peter, and John, said, "All they asked was that we continue to remember the poor, the very thing I was eager to do" (Galatians 2:10).

In chapter 1 I suggested the single truth Jesus communicated in the Good Samaritan is that God expects us to take the initiative, crossing boundaries and overcoming barriers to show His mercy by serving others. How you respond to the needs of others is determined by who you love the most. If you love God most, you will be others-focused, drawn away from a lifestyle of self-centeredness toward the service of others, including the poor.

The challenge of poverty and ministry to the poor is a universal issue-based passion for Christ followers because wholeness—God's concern for the poor, sick, and downtrodden—is a central theme in the gospel of the kingdom. If you love Jesus supremely, what is important to Him will become important to you. Loving the poor was important to Jesus. The more you pursue intimacy with Jesus, the more your heart will be stirred toward compassionate action in service of the poor and needy.

Though it may appear controversial to you at first, I believe a benchmark of intimacy with Jesus is a growing measure of compassion for the poor. David Platt, in his book *Radical: Taking Back Your Faith from the American Dream*, put it like this: "If our lives do not reflect radical compassion for the poor, there is reason to wonder if Christ is really in us at all."[3] The action you take will depend on your giftedness, the thread of the poverty mosaic that surfaces as an issue-based passion fueling your life purpose, and your preferred domain of passionate engagement. But in addition to the unique passions to which you are heartlinked by life-shaping experiences, you can expect God to turn your heart toward the poor.

## FOUR FACES OF POVERTY

Poverty defies simplistic explanations and solutions, especially when considered in a global context. I do not present myself as an expert on this topic, but I've found it helpful to simplify this challenge by looking into the four faces of poverty: crisis, corruption, consequences, and choice. Let's look at each one briefly.

### Poverty Resulting from Crisis

---

For a detailed overview of the devastation produced by the January 2010 earthquake in Haiti and what will be needed going forward, download the Haiti Global Issues Update webinar interview with World Relief from the online store at www.TheMissionExchange .org. This is a free resource.

---

Natural disasters such as earthquakes, typhoons, hurricanes, and tsunamis serve as a magnifying glass, giving us a closer and more focused look at the helplessness of people trying to cope with the aftermath of an "act of God." When the affected communities are already poor, such as Haiti in January 2010, natural disasters amplify their vulnerability. But without a safety net provided by government assistance and private insurance, almost everyone, including those living in a more stable economic condition before a crisis, will need the help of nongovernmental organizations (NGOs) and local churches to rebuild their lives. Most of the world lives beyond the reach of these safety nets and is at the mercy of Good Samaritans like me and you to partner with NGOs and congregations who have the technical expertise needed to provide both relief and development.

Crisis that induces or exacerbates poverty goes beyond acts of God to acts of war. One of the most widely reported examples of war-induced crisis is the Darfur region of southern Sudan. Since 2003 the Jinjawiid militia has embarked on a campaign of murder, rape, threats, and organized starvation that has left more than four hundred thousand dead, and displaced over 2.5 million people.[4]

Armani Tinjany is a twenty-nine-year-old college graduate and school-teacher who told her story to a *Washington Post* reporter. She had lived a comfortable life with her family in a village of stone compounds until the Jinjawiid militia galloped into town. They burned buildings, killed the men, raped the women, and left a once bustling community in smoldering ruins. She fled for her life to a Chadian desert that had been converted into a refugee camp. It was anything but an oasis. She had not seen her husband or parents and had no idea if they made it out alive.[5] Like the man with a sick daughter I met in India, her story is not unique. There are millions just like her in the northern region of the Democratic Republic of Congo, where a second holocaust has claimed five million lives and left many more deeply entrenched in poverty due to the crisis of war fueled by conflict minerals.

## Poverty Resulting from Corruption

Some people, in addition to crisis, are impoverished by corruption, tossed aside like leftovers at the banquet table of the rich and powerful. The prophet Ezekiel spoke to the power brokers in Jerusalem, expressing the righteous anger of God, saying, "The people of the land practice extortion and commit robbery; they oppress the poor and needy and mistreat the alien, denying them justice" (Ezekiel 22:29). We use the saying "where there is smoke, there is fire." Where there is chronic injustice, there is almost always systemic poverty. We'll take a closer look at oppression and injustice in the next chapter.

## Poverty Resulting from Consequences

A common misconception about poverty is that a majority of the poor are reaping the consequences of their own lack of initiative or bad decisions. In fact global poverty is more about the lack of options than poor decisions. Robert Chambers, a British researcher, said it bluntly: "People so close to the edge cannot afford laziness or stupidity. They have to work and work hard, whenever and however they can. Many of the lazy and stupid poor are dead."[6] People who work today to provide food for tonight are far less inclined to "call in sick" for frivolous reasons tomorrow.

I am not suggesting that personal responsibility is irrelevant to this conversation. Some people are poor because of ill-advised or even sinful choices. Alcoholism and drug abuse are like economic parasites that ravage the creativity and productivity of addicts. Even value neutral but self-defeating decisions such as dropping out of high school can put people on a steep incline that greatly impedes their social progress. Out-of-wedlock pregnancies, criminal activity, and other missteps are speed bumps that slow the journey of upward mobility. To state it positively, in the United States today, one who completes high school, does not have a child out of wedlock, marries and remains married is very unlikely to be poor.[7]

Even when poverty results from the logical consequences of poor choices, Jesus compels us to show mercy and compassion. Who among us would not admit that but for the grace of God, there go I? We are commanded to love others who don't like us, can't repay us, and won't thank us. This kind of Good Samaritan activity is not easy; or as we discovered in Luke 6:27-36, we will need grace for that.

## Poverty Resulting from Choice

The final face of poverty, and seemingly least relevant for this conversation, is those who are poor by choice. We often describe people in this category as having taken a vow of poverty, embracing the simplest of lifestyles. Speaking of Lady Poverty, Francis of Assisi told his comrades, "I am about to take a wife of surpassing fairness."[8] He believed he was following in the footsteps of Jesus, who chose a simpler path, saying, "Foxes have holes and birds of the air have nests, but the Son of Man has no place to lay his head" (Luke 9:58). Few in the Protestant tradition have embraced this calling, nor do we spend a lot of time reflecting on the implications of Jesus' instructions to the rich ruler, saying, "Sell everything you have and give to the poor, and you will have treasure in heaven. Then come, follow me" (Luke 18:22). I believe there are veins of truth we can mine from those who have embraced poverty by choice and will revisit this idea later in the chapter.

## STUPID DEATH

---

To explore the stupid death caused by HIV/AIDS, consider downloading the Global Status of HIV/AIDS webinar interview with World Relief from the online store at www.TheMissionExchange .org. Use the one-time discount code chapter7-neighbor to download this Global Issues Update webinar for free.

---

One of the most captivating images from the January 2010 earthquake in Haiti was the rescue of a seven-year-old girl buried in the rubble of her collapsed house, captured live on CNN. Rescue workers heard the girl's cries for help and dug through the debris only to discover her right leg was trapped. Millions watched the fear, agony, and pain on her face, while workers struggled to decide if they should amputate her leg or keep working to remove the remnants of the fallen structure. Once freed from the rubble, she was transferred to a first-aid station that did not have the capacity to deal with her injuries. She died about an hour after being rescued before she was able to receive treatment at a better-equipped facility outside the city. I remember looking into this little girl's face as her mother stroked her hair and whispered comforting words into her ear. I had a similar life-shaping experience that heartlinked me to poor children in India more than fifteen years earlier. But this time I was sitting at my kitchen table, trying to decide if it was immoral to eat my dinner while watching something so tragic unfold in real time. This is the power and complexity of a connected world.

CNN journalist Anderson Cooper was one of the reporters covering this story. In an interview with Larry King, he described what was happening:

There's just stupid death happening here now. It doesn't have to happen, and it's really upsetting to see. A little girl is dying because her leg was crushed. Someone doesn't have to die of that. A leg can be amputated if there's a doctor there to do it. If there's an infection, they can take antibiotics to be treated. It doesn't have to spread through the body and kill somebody. It's really stupid. It's infuriating. People died today who did not need to die. People will die tonight, in the next hour, who do not need to die.[9]

We live in a world filled with stupid death, and it strikes the poor more than anyone. For the more than 3.5 billion people who live on less than $2 a day, poverty is like an accelerant for a raging fire, increasing the chances they will die prematurely of starvation or preventable disease. Approximately twenty-five thousand people die every day of hunger-related causes.[10] Another five million die annually from water-related illnesses.[11] In Africa, 165 of every one thousand children born will die before their fifth birthday. And almost all of it is stupid death, ranging from diarrheal diseases (17 percent) to malaria (8 percent) to AIDS (3 percent).[12]

The World Health Organization reports there are over five hundred million cases of malaria annually, resulting in 1.5 to 2.7 million deaths. Though few of us in the West ever think about it unless traveling to an "exotic" location, some scientists have postulated that one out of every two people who have ever lived have died of malaria.[13] This one-celled parasite, known as plasmodia, may be the poster child for stupid death, considering medicines are available to stop the progression of the disease and a mosquito net costing $10 greatly reduces the risk of getting it.

The AIDS pandemic, especially in Africa, is nearly impossible to put in a context that is comprehensible. This treatable but incurable disease kills eight thousand people every day. Like a hurricane-force tidal wave, it is leaving a wake of orphans, mostly in sub-Saharan Africa and Asia, projected to reach twenty-five million in 2010.[14] In an attempt to put this tragedy in perspective, Richard Stearns describes a chain of children holding hands and stretching out across America. This chain, starting in New York, would stretch all the way to Seattle, back to Philadelphia, back to San Francisco, then east to Washington, D.C., back again to Los Angeles, and finally to about Kansas City—more than five and a half times across the United States![15]

## MONEY VERSUS PROPERTY

Life in a connected world puts stupid death on the side of the road in a way that cannot be ignored. One of the four faces of poverty is those who are poor by choice. I am not campaigning for a revival of asceticism accompanied by a vow of poverty, but I do believe we can learn an important lesson from this stream of spirituality about how to embrace a lifestyle of simplicity. Living a simple lifestyle does not mean arbitrary limits on income or net worth, nor does it generate a uniform list of what Jesus would eat, wear, or drive. I know this subject deserves a much fuller treatment than is appropriate here, but I want to highlight one specific worldview shift that fosters simplicity and opens a gateway to generosity and compassionate action on behalf of those suffering in poverty.

The Bible clearly teaches that we are stewards and managers of what God has entrusted to us. Though we struggle to apply this principle, most Christ followers would acknowledge all we have comes from God and belongs to God. But practically speaking we live as if stewardship applies to our money but not our property, as if cash that has been converted into stuff belongs to us.

Imagine the following example. You spend a few hours online paying bills and balancing your checkbook and are pleasantly surprised to discover an unexpected cushion of $600 after your tithe and savings. (I know you may find that hard to picture, but as I said, imagine.) You have been eying a sale on flat-screen televisions for some time and know you can purchase one for $595. In a matter of hours you have converted cash into stuff and are enjoying a movie in full HD with popcorn in the comfort of your living room.

The next morning while making coffee, you turn on the new big screen to watch the news before heading off to work, only to discover a 7.0 magnitude earthquake ravaged Haiti, leaving more than one hundred thousand people dead and two million homeless. An already stumbling economy has been brought to its knees. Before the day is over you have received emergency appeals from trusted relief and development organizations along with a dozen Facebook status updates from friends pointing you toward practical ways to help. And you know they are not exaggerating because you can see the destruction in real time, with full HD.

For most of us, one idea that would never even enter our minds while sorting out how to respond to this tragedy is that God might actually want us to return the television in order to free up funds that could be used to help. We view money differently than property. Forget about recent purchases and just think about all the "stuff" in your house (never mind the garage). How could any of us really look into the face of poverty, whether caused by crisis, corruption, or logical consequences, and say I can't afford to do anything to help? God's ownership stake does not end the moment cash is traded for a sales receipt. In spite of the fact that our connected world, with online services such as Craigslist and eBay, has made it easier than ever to turn stuff back into cash, we tend to view money very differently than property, and it greatly limits our options.

This is an unbiblical worldview when contrasted to how the early church viewed property. "There were no needy persons among them. From time to time those who owned lands or houses sold them, brought the money from the sales and put it at the apostles' feet, and it was distributed to anyone as he had need" (Acts 4:34-35). The apostle John would later write, "If anyone has *material possessions* and sees his brother in need but has no pity on him, how can the love of God be in him? Dear children, let us not love with words or tongue but with actions and in truth" (1 John 3:17-18). Perhaps we have too quickly and easily taken the exit ramps of rationalization and justification enabling us to pass by on the other side.

We quote Psalm 50:10, affirming God owns "the cattle on a thousand hills" as a word of encouragement that He is not at a loss in providing for *our needs*. That is true. But in an agrarian society, cattle represented a business owner's inventory. We might paraphrase that verse for our time, saying, "God owns the inventory in a thousand warehouses." Why is that important? Because this verse says as much about God's ownership stake (100 percent) in my property as it does about His commitment to my prosperity. Every time our connected world offers us the opportunity to be Good Samaritans, we need to prayerfully process the decision about involvement based on total inventory, not just available money. This subtle but powerful change in worldview opens the door to a life of open-handed simplicity and generosity, empowering us to engage more deeply with the issue-based passion of poverty.

## PRAY LIKE A ROCK STAR

On February 2, 2006, Bono, the front man and lead singer of U2, addressed the group gathered for the annual prayer breakfast in Washington, D.C. Just a few brief excerpts from this unlikely prophet left me wanting to pray, and serve, like a rock star:

God is in the slums, in the cardboard boxes where the poor play house. God is in the silence of a mother who has infected her child with a virus that will end both their lives. God is in the cries heard under the rubble of war. God is in the debris of wasted opportunity and lives, and God is with us if we are with them.

"If you remove the yoke from your midst, the pointing of the finger and the speaking of wickedness, and if you give yourself to the hungry and satisfy the desire of the afflicted, then your light will rise in darkness and your gloom will become like midday and the Lord will continually guide you and satisfy your desire even in scorched places.". . .

And finally . . . this is not about charity in the end, is it? It's about justice. . . . Africa makes a fool of our idea of justice; it makes a farce of our idea of equality. It mocks our pieties; it doubts our concern, and it questions our commitment. Six and a half thousand Africans are still dying every day of a preventable, treatable disease, for lack of drugs we can buy at any drug store. This is not about charity, this is about Justice and Equality.

Because there's no way we can look at what's happening in Africa and, if we're honest, conclude that deep down, we would let it happen anywhere else – if we really accepted that Africans are equal to us. . . . Look what happened in South East Asia with the tsunami. One hundred fifty thousand lives lost[16] to the misnomer of all misnomers, "mother nature." In Africa, 150,000 lives are lost every month – a tsunami every month. And it's a completely avoidable catastrophe.

It's annoying, but justice and equality are mates, aren't they? Justice always wants to hang out with equality. And equality is a real pain. . . .

Preventing the poorest of the poor from selling their products while we sing the virtues of the free market . . . that's a justice issue. Holding children to ransom for the debts of their grandparents . . . that's a justice issue. Withholding life-saving medicines out of deference to the Office of Patents . . . that's a justice issue.[17]

A few weeks before his prayer breakfast speech, Bono challenged our generation to be history makers on behalf of the poor:

We can be the generation that no longer accepts that an accident of latitude determines whether a child lives or dies—but will we be that generation? Will we in the West realize our potential or will we sleep in the comfort of our affluence with apathy and indifference murmuring softly in our ears? Fifteen thousand people dying needlessly every day from AIDS, TB, and malaria. Mothers, fathers, teachers, farmers, nurses, mechanics, children. This is Africa's crisis. That it's not on the nightly news, that we do not treat this as an emergency—that's our crisis.

Future generations . . . will know whether we answered the question. The evidence will be the world around them. History will be our judge, but what's written is up to us. We can't say our generation couldn't afford it. And we can't say our generation didn't have reason to do it. It's up to us.[18]

Everyone has the same need for food; not everyone has the same access to provision.

Chapter 8

# GOD'S PASSION FOR THE OPPRESSED

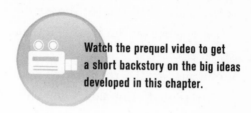

Watch the prequel video to get
a short backstory on the big ideas
developed in this chapter.

Everyone has the same need for freedom, but not everyone has the same access to justice. By *freedom* I am not referring to democracy or capitalism but to a liberty that transcends economics and politics. Freedom in this sense is a self-evident truth that all people are the image-bearers of God, who created them. In the words of Thomas Jefferson, we have been "endowed with certain unalienable rights," including not only the right to live, but to do so in freedom. Liberty is a human right, rooted in eternal rather than civil authority. As a plant needs sunlight, rain, and nutrients from the soil, we need freedom in order to blossom, flourish, and reflect the beautiful fruitfulness intended by our Creator. Everyone has the same need for freedom; not everyone has the same access to justice.

In 1983 I was arrested, twice, for the same crime in less than two months. Though I've done many things in my past to make you think less of me, this is probably not one of them. I was part of a short-term mission team serving in a Muslim country in Asia. Our primary focus was selling Bibles and books about life based on the teachings of Jesus from store to store in major cities. All the material had been printed locally, and though we had been advised that distributing it freely would be problematic, it was perfectly legal to sell. At least that's what we thought. We memorized some phrases and took to the streets.

The first time our team got arrested, the charges were dismissed within two days and we were asked to leave the city by officials in the police department. The circumstances surrounding our release were every bit as miraculous to me as anything I read in the book of Acts, minus the shaking of the prison and angelic escort (see Acts 12 and 16), but that is another story. The second go-around was more by the book, including fingerprints and mug shots along with an official ruling by a judge. We were sentenced, one by one, to three months in jail. But the judge commuted the sentence on the condition that we agreed to pack up our van and leave the country.

During our first incarceration we were in a holding area with a handful of other alleged criminals. One who spoke just enough English to communicate was a Palestinian whose Egyptian passport had been stolen. He claimed he had done nothing wrong, but the embassy was unwilling to come to his aid. I'm sure there was more to his story than he could communicate in broken English, and it is very possible he had given the authorities more reason to arrest him than failure to produce valid documents. But I remember the moment I realized this man was not only homeless but "nationless,"[1] without anyone to advocate on his behalf. With a mixture of fatalism and despair, he said, "I don't know what will happen to me."

When our team was arrested the second time just a few weeks later, from the moment we were taken into custody, our embassies were notified (one member of our team was Canadian). We knew we received special treatment because they cleared out a small room in the police station to avoid putting us in the common holding area with other prisoners. They allowed us to bring in items from our van, and even though we had to pay for it ourselves, they served us food brought in from outside the jail. The judge was creative in seeking a win-win solution that would enable him to declare us guilty, impose a "harsh sentence," and still send us packing out of the country as "free men."

In reflecting on the differences between our team and the Palestinian I met in jail, I have come to realize that for millions of people around the world, such as the Dalits of South Asia or children trapped in bonded labor or prostitution, Lady Justice is not only blind but deaf and dumb. In the words of King Solomon, "If you see the poor oppressed in a district, and justice and rights denied, do not be surprised at such things; for one official is eyed by a higher one, and over them both are others higher still" (Ecclesiastes 5:8). To put it in the context of Western culture, Lady Justice is too often like the popular, good-looking, rich girl you remember from high school who ignored most, used some, and played favorites with a few, based on her own fickle desires.

## THE GOD OF THE OPPRESSED

There is a sense in which poverty is the younger sibling of injustice. As Bono described it so passionately, solving the dilemma of poverty almost always calls for more than charity; it's about justice. I could fill up this entire chapter with verses demonstrating God's selective emphasis in the Bible on justice, with special concern for aliens, orphans, and widows. Isaiah warned, "Woe to those who make unjust laws, to those who issue oppressive decrees, to deprive the poor of their rights and withhold justice from the oppressed of my people, making widows their prey and robbing the fatherless" (Isaiah 10:1-2).

One of the most quoted verses from the first chapter of Isaiah says, "'Come now, let us reason together,' says the LORD. 'Though your sins are like scarlet, they shall be as white as snow; though they are red as crimson, they shall be like wool'" (Isaiah 1:18). This is one of the most beautiful and captivating images of God's forgiveness, which we rightly apply to our own spiritual journey. But rarely do we stop to explore the context of the passage, asking "Whose sins?" Isaiah is comparing the sins of Judah with the sins of Sodom and Gomorrah. What sins? We can answer that by looking at the previous verse and noting what they were failing to do: "Stop doing wrong, learn to do right! Seek justice, encourage the oppressed. Defend the cause of the fatherless, plead the case of the widow" (Isaiah 1:16-17).

Zechariah challenged the remnant of Jews who had returned to Jerusalem from their captivity in Babylon to "Administer true justice; show mercy and compassion to one another. Do not oppress the widow or the fatherless, the alien or the poor. In your hearts do not think evil of each other" (Zechariah 7:9-10). And Lemuel, one of the authors of Proverbs, taught the people of God to "Speak up for those who cannot speak for themselves, for the rights of all who are destitute. Speak up and judge fairly; defend the rights of the poor and needy" (Proverbs 31:8-9).

Jesus declared His mission in the synagogue in Nazareth, quoting from Isaiah, saying, "He has sent me to proclaim freedom for the prisoners and recovery of sight for the blind, to release the oppressed" (Luke 4:18). He later said, "Come to me, all you who are weary and burdened, and I will give you rest. Take my yoke upon you and learn from me, for I am gentle and humble in heart, and you will find rest for your souls. For my yoke is easy and my burden is light" (Matthew 11:28-30). We hear the phrase "weary and burdened" and think about the stress level produced by our job or the frustrations of a high-volume commute. And I'm thankful anyone who comes to Jesus will find rest for a weary soul. But these words are especially meaningful to the child prostitute in Bangkok and the bonded laborer in India.

When the Israelites groaned in their slavery and cried out for help, "God heard their groaning and he remembered his covenant with Abraham, with Isaac and with Jacob. So God looked on the Israelites and was concerned about them" (Exodus 2:24-25). Saying God "remembered his covenant" does not suggest God forgot what He had promised. It is reinforcing that what God is about to do in setting captives free is rooted in or a fulfillment of the promise made to the patriarchs in the Abrahamic covenant. Though the promise was made to Abraham and later affirmed to both Isaac and Jacob, it was clearly stated that the blessing would extend to "all peoples on earth" (Genesis 12:3).

The ultimate fulfillment of that promised blessing came in the ministry of Jesus, whose kingdom message includes freedom and deliverance from spiritual bondage or demonic chains, and reinforces God's compassion for those on the wrong side of unjust power. Standing against oppression and injustice is a universal issue-based passion for Christ followers that is rooted in the gospel of the kingdom. God's highest priority is clearly to set us free from the power of sin and death. We'll focus on that in the next chapter. Life in a fallen world, marred by sin, where power struggles and greed infect rich and poor alike, will leave us battling against injustice until Jesus returns to make all things new. Until then, the more you become like Jesus, the more you become a friend of God, the more self-directed energy you will find to learn more about, engage with, and influence others toward justice-related causes, even when sacrifice is required. And every time a Christ follower speaks out against injustice, we proclaim the gospel of the kingdom led by a King committed to set captives free.

## LOSS VERSUS RISK

The Holy Spirit clearly guided the authors of the Scripture to selectively emphasize aliens, widows, and orphans as deserving of special attention and protection. James, echoing the voices of Old Testament prophets, said, "Religion that God our Father accepts as pure and faultless is this: to look after orphans and widows in their distress and to keep oneself from being polluted by the world" (James 1:27). Perhaps these individuals were highlighted because the loss of a husband or parents or migration to a new land produces a special category of risk instead of loss. God cares about the sorrow that accompanies losses of this nature, but the elevation of foreigners, widows, the fatherless, and orphans to a place of special concern in the eyes of God is based on their increased vulnerability to exploitation. Apparently there were questions about this issue in the church at Ephesus, which Paul addressed in his letter to Timothy, offering specific guidelines and qualifications for the church's responsibility to care for widows (see 1 Timothy 5:1-16).

What does religion that God accepts as "pure and faultless" look like today? Or to put it another way, who in our global village is in the spotlight of God's compassion due to increased vulnerability and the risk of oppression? In the most general terms, not much has changed. The poor are still more vulnerable than the rich. Outsiders (foreigners) are more vulnerable than insiders. Women are more vulnerable than men, especially in the developing world. Widows are more vulnerable than other women. Children are more vulnerable than adults. Fatherless children and orphans are more vulnerable than other children. The girl child is more vulnerable than her brothers.

---

To explore the unique vulnerability of women and girls globally, consider downloading the Global Status of Women at Risk webinar interview with Sisters in Service from the online store at www .TheMissionExchange.org. Use the one-time discount code chapter8#1-neighbor to download this Global Issues Update webinar for free.

---

I often hear people say following Jesus is not about religion but about relationship, and I agree. True religion is characterized by a growing measure of intimacy with God. Greater intimacy with God produces a greater sense of responsibility for the most vulnerable because they are in the spotlight of His compassion. Practically speaking, what does that look like today? The answer deserves more space than I can give here. But let's begin the conversation with a look at four links in the chain of oppression and injustice that disproportionately impact the poor, outsiders, women, the fatherless, and orphans.

## FOUR LINKS IN THE CHAIN OF INJUSTICE AND OPPRESSION

### Illegal Land Seizure

Illegal land seizure is the forcible acquisition of property in the absence of any land titles or agreement between the rightful owner and the person taking over the land. While at times this illegal action is taken by business or government leaders who are abusing their authority, it also happens with in-laws or other relatives when women are left to fend for themselves after the death of their husbands. Given the AIDS pandemic in sub-Saharan Africa and Asia, many widows and orphans have been the victims of illegal land seizure. In Uganda, only 5 percent of the land occupied by nationals has a land title. This greatly exacerbates the problem widows face in settling property disputes. According to Human Rights Watch, Kenyan women constitute 80 percent of the agricultural labor force and provide 60 percent of farm income, yet own only 5 percent of the land.[2]

This is not a new problem, and the Bible clearly reveals how God feels about it. In 1 Kings 21 we are told the story of King Ahab who wanted to plant a vegetable garden on property that was conveniently located near his palace. He met with Naboth, the property owner, offering to either purchase the land or trade it for something better. But when Naboth chose not to sell the inheritance of his forefathers, King Ahab "went home, sullen and angry" (1 Kings 21:4). His wicked wife, Jezebel, hatched a plot to cheer up her husband, hiring scoundrels to falsely accuse Naboth of cursing both God and the king. They did as the queen had instructed and took Naboth "outside the city and stoned him to death" (1 Kings 21:13). Naboth's property was illegally seized, and he was put to death, but God was watching. Elijah rebuked the king and pronounced God's judgment on him.

## Bonded Slavery

It has been said that slavery is not legal anywhere but happens everywhere.[3] William Wilberforce and his network of collaborators did not eradicate slavery; they changed the way the world thinks about it and made it much more difficult to defend. Estimates of modern-day slavery range from twelve million[4] to twenty-seven million.[5] The United Nations Working Group on Contemporary Forms of Slavery estimated twenty million people were trapped in bonded slavery as far back as 1999. Human Rights Watch estimates there are as many as fifteen million children in bonded slavery in India alone; approximately two-thirds of today's slaves are in South Asia.[6]

Bonded slaves are owned by an employer as part of a debt repayment process, and their continual labor is required to pay the interest on the debt. They are often forced to work in extremely harsh conditions seven days a week with no rights and few, if any, breaks. Their meager wage, if any at all, is well below what is needed to pay down the debt due to exorbitant interest rates. The unpaid debt is passed down like a negative inheritance enslaving families for generations.

Millions of poor families, living on as little as $2 per day, are one emergency away from falling into the trap of bonded labor. In desperation they seek a small loan to secure immediate funds with the promise to work for the lender to pay back the principal with interest. But the interest on the loan is so much higher than the wage that it is impossible to repay the compounding debt. A disproportionate percentage of bonded slaves are children. They are easily manipulated, often threatened, beaten, and abused. God has clearly spoken against this form of slavery, saying, "I will be quick to testify against . . . those who defraud laborers of their wages, who oppress the widows and the fatherless, and deprive aliens of justice, but do not fear me" (Malachi 3:5).

Thirteen-year-old Renise was a victim of a unique form of child slavery, and her story is a reminder of the fact that God can bring good out of tragedy. Ironically, for Renise, the 2010 earthquake in Haiti was a blessing that ended a childhood of abuse when she was picked up by rescue workers on the streets of Port-au-Prince. Driven by extreme poverty and their inability to care for her, Renise's parents had given her away as a *resavek*, a Creole word meaning "stays with," such as one who stays with but is not part of the family. In addition to long hours of domestic labor, resaveks are often abused. Several months before the earthquake, Renise was raped and became pregnant. She told her story to *60 Minutes* correspondent Scott Pelley:

"There were moments when I would just stop and cry. I cried because they made me work like a donkey. Their daughter never picked up one bucket when I was there. Not once." She said the family didn't treat her like their daughter. "I used to sleep on the floor."[7]

---

To explore the unique vulnerability associated with street children globally, consider downloading the Global Status of Street Children webinar interview with Viva Network from the online store at www.TheMissionExchange.org. Use the one-time discount code chapter8#2-neighbor to download this Global Issues Update webinar for free.

---

Even before the earthquake, more than 75 percent of Port-au-Prince dwellings had no running water on the premises. People had to fetch water from public fountains and stand pipes, often several kilometers away. Resaveks such as Renise often begin their day early and end it late, carrying water for the families with whom they are staying. In between they look after younger children, clean the house, and do laundry. Renise was rescued after the earthquake and put in the care of an organization called Global Orphan. They are working with a Haitian family to facilitate a legitimate adoption. Hers is a story of beauty for ashes, but fears are high that the thousands of children who have become fatherless, orphaned, or separated from their families by the Haiti earthquake will be quickly absorbed into the shadows as resaveks.

## Refugees

According to a June 2009 UN High Commission for Refugees (UNHCR) press release, there are sixteen million refugees and another twenty-six million people in refugee or refugee-like situations.[8] By UNHCR definition, a refugee is a person who, based on a well-founded fear of persecution due to race, religion, nationality, membership in a social group, or political opinion, has fled his or her country of nationality and is unable to or unwilling to avail himself or herself of the protection of that country. People who for similar reasons are residing away from their homes but within their countries of origin are referred to as Internally Displaced Persons (IDP). It all sounds like legal mumbo jumbo until, like twenty-eight-year-old Armani Tinjany, who we met in the last chapter, your world is turned upside down by Jinjawiid militia, and you are running for your life or eking out an existence in the squalor of a refugee camp.

The unique vulnerability of refugees, the "aliens and strangers" of our time, is reinforced for me almost every day. The Mission Exchange is headquartered in the Atlanta affiliate office of World Relief, one of twenty-three such local affiliates in the United States that is focused specifically on refugee resettlement. On any given day the lobby one floor above my office is bustling with people who have recently arrived from refugee camps around the world and are beginning the daunting process of establishing themselves in the United States. Recently I had the chance to sit down with a young man from Eritrea who had been resettled by World Relief. He told me a harrowing story that stretched over ten years and three countries, including prison beatings, escapes, and all-night marches through the dangerous countryside. There are tens of thousands like him still waiting in refugee camps or running from horrible circumstances, hoping to begin anew somewhere else.

---

To learn more about forcibly displaced peoples, consider downloading the Global Status of Refugees webinar interview with International Association for Refugees founder Tom Albinson from the online store at www.TheMissionExchange.org. Use the one-time discount code chapter8#3-neighbor to download this Global Issues Update webinar for free.

---

## Human Trafficking and the Global Sex Trade

Human trafficking is the third largest (after drugs and weapons) and fastest growing criminal industry in the world, with a total market value of over $32 billion.[9] It is estimated that between 600,000 and 800,000 children, women, and men are trafficked across international borders annually, with 80 percent of the victims being women and young girls and 50 percent minors. This massive global enterprise preys on the most vulnerable using abduction, coercion, and deception. Forced prostitution and rape for profit is a lucrative business fueled by the lust and depravity of men, including thousands from Europe and the United States who travel to Asia on "sexcations."

I interviewed Jim Martin, national director of Church Mobilization for International Justice Mission (IJM), on the subject of human trafficking for the June 2009 *Global Issues Update*, a bimonthly resource provided by the organization I'm privileged to lead, The Mission Exchange. In that interview, Jim shared the following powerful story that personalizes the overwhelming statistics of the global sex trade.

To learn more about the issue of human trafficking, consider down-loading the Global Status of Human Trafficking webinar interview with International Justice Mission from the online store at www.TheMissionExchange.org. Use the one-time discount code chapter8#4-neighbor to download this Global Issues Update webinar for free.

Elizabeth is from an ethnic minority in a country in South Asia. She had just finished tenth grade in school when she was approached by a neighbor who told Elizabeth she could get her a good job in another city, just across the border from her home country. As the oldest of seven children, she felt a measure of responsibility for the well-being of her family. She was from a Christian home and hoped to attend Bible college in the future. In spite of her fear of traveling and venturing into the unknown, Elizabeth jumped at this opportunity to help her family and save money to further her education.

Inexperienced and vulnerable, Elizabeth was sold through a trafficker to a brothel owner upon arriving in the new city. She was told by the brothel owner that she would have to prostitute herself to repay the expenses he had incurred to purchase her from the trafficker. Elizabeth, horrified and repulsed by this proposition, refused to cooperate. In return she was locked alone in a small room and given only enough food and water to keep her alive. After weeks of emotional and psychological abuse, Elizabeth gave in to the demands of the brothel owner.

Her first John was a westerner who paid $240 to rape her because she was a virgin. Elizabeth found herself sinking deeper into a labyrinth of shame and sexual exploitation. The emotional pain and disgust she felt pushed her to the brink of suicide, but she decided to keep crying out to God for help. Elizabeth even enlisted the other girls in the brothel to join her in prayer, but they mocked her invitation, saying, "Don't you know God can't hear prayers from a place like this?"

Unbeknownst to Elizabeth, while she was praying, an IJM investigator was able to infiltrate this brothel and document specific information for local authorities who conducted a raid that liberated Elizabeth and the others with her. Based on additional information Elizabeth was able to provide, twenty-eight more girls were also rescued. The momentum associated with these raids and convictions virtually flushed traffickers and sex traders from the area.

When IJM rescuers found the room in which Elizabeth had been trapped and serially raped for profit, they found these words from Psalm 27:1-3 written on the wall in her handwriting:

The Lord is my light and my salvation; whom shall I fear? the Lord is the strength of my life; of whom shall I be afraid? When the wicked, even mine enemies and my foes, came upon me to eat up my flesh, they stumbled and fell. Though an host should encamp against me, my heart shall not fear: though war should rise against me, in this will I be confident. (KJV)

 God heard Elizabeth's prayers and used individuals like me and you who support ministries such as IJM to be the hands and feet of Jesus, "to proclaim freedom for the prisoners . . . to release the oppressed, to proclaim the year of the Lord's favor" (Luke 4:18-19). Everyone has the same need for freedom; not everyone has the same access to justice.

Chapter 9

# GOD'S PASSION FOR THE LOST

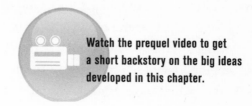

Watch the prequel video to get
a short backstory on the big ideas
developed in this chapter.

Everyone has the same need for forgiveness, but not everyone has the same access to the gospel. Every hour of every day, in every language, "the heavens declare the glory of God" (Psalm 19:1). Even in its fallen state, while groaning for its own redemption, creation is a faithful witness, proclaiming that God is. But it doesn't explain that His name is Jesus; it doesn't say He came with a mission to preach good news to the poor, proclaim freedom for the prisoners, and release the oppressed. The Bible is very clear in stating, "all have sinned and fall short of the glory of God" (Romans 3:23). But all have not heard the good news: "And how can they hear without someone preaching to them?" (Romans 10:14). Everyone has the same need for forgiveness; not everyone has the same access to the gospel.

A few weeks before I was arrested in the summer of 1983, I had a life-shaping experience that heartlinked me to lost people, especially those who have not heard. As I mentioned in the last chapter, the short-term mission team on which I served was primarily selling books based on the teachings of Jesus along with Bibles, in a Muslim country in Asia. I had worked hard to memorize phrases in the local language and was growing in confidence as it relates to making my pitch: "Hi, my name is Steve. I'm a student from America, and I'm visiting here for the summer. I have some books for sale that I think might interest you. Would you like to see them?"

I prayed before I went in a store, asking God to give me favor, and I viewed each interaction as an opportunity to show God's love. But like a good salesman, I would typically begin pulling books out of my shoulder bag and displaying them on the counter before the person had opportunity to say no. I tried hard to avoid coming across pushy by exuding positivity. I discovered eye contact and a big smile bought me more than enough time to get several of the books out of the bag.

One hot afternoon I made my way into a small neighborhood grocery store, hoping I could sell some books to the person at the counter. To my delight the cashier was a student, several years younger than me, probably still in high school. I went up to the counter looking to strike up a friendship and ultimately put some thought-provoking materials into the hands of a Muslim family. I shared my phrases, displayed my books, and smiled as genuinely as ever from ear to ear. But the young man behind the counter looked at me as if I were an alien who had just landed from outer space. He shrugged his shoulders and extended both arms, bent at the elbow with palms up, in a universal pantomime that says, "I don't get it." I repeated my phrases, slowly. He put one hand over his chest and extended the other with the palm facing me, using a waving good-bye motion that culturally communicated a gracious no thank you.

We were the only people in the store, so I packed up my books deliberately, one by one, as if to say, "I'm going to give you one more chance to change your mind." He didn't. In a moment of social awkwardness that I hadn't experienced since middle school, magnified by the cultural and language barriers, I made my way back to the door. As I stepped down to the sidewalk, the spring-loaded door slammed behind me, and a simple yet profound thought went through my mind: *What if that was the only chance he will ever have to be exposed to the gospel?* I remember the feeling of injustice that washed over me and the cocktail of emotions ranging from anger to sadness to grief.

I was so arrested by the experience that I wandered to a nearby park and sat down on a bench. Several children were playing in my field of view. I was struck by the high probability that these little kids would grow up, live their lives, and move on into eternity without ever having a meaningful opportunity to hear the good news. I began thinking back to all the advantages I had growing up with godly parents and the fact that I could not remember a time I did not know Jesus loved me. To paraphrase Bono, "Why should an accident of latitude determine whether a child hears or doesn't hear the good news?" Though I would not have described it in these words, I realized perhaps for the first time that everyone has the same need for forgiveness, but not everyone has the same access to the gospel.

---

To learn more about the challenge and opportunity of reaching oral learners, consider downloading the webinar *Making Disciples of Oral Learners—Truth That Sticks*, with Avery Willis, from the online store at www.TheMissionExchange.org. Use the one-time discount code chapter9#1-neighbor to download this webinar for free.

---

## THE GOD WHO SEEKS

Jesus publically declared His mission in the synagogue in Nazareth, and He based decisions on future ministry, such as the opportunity to remain in Capernaum, on the reason He was sent. He later spoke with even greater clarity about His life purpose, saying, "For the Son of Man came to seek and to save what was lost" (Luke 19:10). The metaphor of "lost" and "found" was used repeatedly by Jesus when speaking of salvation. Nowhere do we see that more clearly and powerfully communicated than the three parables in Luke 15.

Jesus told these stories to a group of Pharisees who were disgusted by the fact that He was a friend of sinners. The three stories have a common element in that something is lost (coin, sheep, son), what is lost is found, and they all end with a time of celebration. But there is a not so obvious yet very important difference between the third story and the other two. Here's how Timothy Keller describes it in his book *The Prodigal God*:

In the first two someone "goes out" and searches diligently for that which is lost. The searchers let nothing distract them or stand in their way. By the time we get to the third story, and we hear about the plight of the lost son, we are fully prepared to expect that someone will set out to search for him. No one does. It is startling, and Jesus meant it to be so. By placing the three parables so closely together, he is inviting thoughtful listeners to ask: "Well, who should have gone out and searched for the lost son?" Jesus knew the Bible thoroughly, and he knew that at its very beginning it tells another story of an elder brother and younger brother—Cain and Abel. In that story, God tells the resentful and proud older brother: "*You* are your brother's keeper."[1]

Keller goes on to say what a true elder brother would have done: "He would have said, 'Father, my younger brother has been a fool, and now his life is in ruins. But I will go look for him and bring him home. And if the inheritance is gone—as I expect it is—I'll bring him back in to the family at my expense."[2] By putting a flawed elder brother in the story, Jesus amplifies the yearning in our hearts for a true one. And in Jesus we have a "firstborn among many brothers" (Romans 8:29). We are of the same family, so Jesus is not ashamed to call us brothers (see Hebrews 2:11). He is the faithful and true elder brother, one who is committed to "seek and save that which was lost." Jesus calls us to follow in His steps, not as Saviors but as messengers. Lost people represent the highest priority passion of Jesus, and as Christ followers we are compelled to join Him in a relentless search.

## THE "JESUS DIED FOR ME" BLIND SPOT

In 1989 I spent three weeks studying Chinese on a university campus in southeast China, one month after the student demonstrations in Tiananmen Square. There were far fewer students on campus that summer, but it wasn't hard to strike up a friendship with the ones who remained. In a laid-back conversation with a group of students one afternoon, I discovered a blind spot in my worldview that greatly impacted how I read the Bible.

Chinese culture gives priority to the group over the individual, and the students had a hard time understanding some of the behaviors they had heard about in America. They asked me, "Is it true some college students in America get an apartment and live in it all by themselves?" When I answered yes, they were dumbfounded, wondering out loud why anyone would choose to live alone. I told them I had lived in an apartment by myself for several years as a college student because I wanted privacy, something they struggled to comprehend. They laughed, admitting my behavior was weird.

They asked a follow-up question: "Is it true some American teenagers get a job and then keep the money for themselves, instead of giving it to the family?" Again, my answer was affirmative, and they were equally surprised. All of a sudden I started to understand why ordering a meal with my Chinese friends in a restaurant was always a group decision and served family style. There weren't even individual meal options on the menu. (Chinese culture is still communal, but the impact of a connected world on young people, especially in urban settings, has begun to produce an increasingly uniform global youth culture.) For the first time in my life, I began to understand that our value for the individual is not universal.

Once that blind spot was exposed, I began to realize how it had colored my reading of the Bible. For years I had read passages such as the Lord's Prayer—"give *us* each day *our* daily bread . . . forgive *us our* sins . . . lead *us* not into temptation"—but all along I was thinking "give *me* (or me and my family) our daily bread . . . forgive *me* for my sins . . . lead *me* not into temptation" (see Luke 11:2-4). The biggest paradigm shift came when I realized Jesus didn't die for me: "He is the atoning sacrifice for our sins, and not only for ours but also for the sins of the whole world" (1 John 2:2). Jesus didn't die for you. He died for everyone.

You might be tempted to categorize this distinction as theological hairsplitting, but hang with me for a moment. This culturally programmed blind spot predisposes us to focus on people instead of peoples. And there is an important difference. God made a covenant promise to Abraham, saying, "All peoples on earth will be blessed through you" (Genesis 12:3). The word *people* is already plural, but God spoke of peoples or nations, not individuals. There is no doubt this promise given first to Abraham, later reaffirmed to Isaac (see Genesis 26:4) and Jacob (see Genesis 28:13-15), is fulfilled in the ministry of Jesus. Paul spoke of this promise to Abraham, saying, "The Scripture foresaw that God would justify the Gentiles [nations] by faith, and announced the gospel in advance to Abraham: 'All nations will be blessed through you'" (Galatians 3:8).

God is passionate about the lost, but not only from the perspective of individuals; He wants to bring as many individuals as possible from all the *nations* to Himself. Jesus repeated this emphasis, challenging His first followers to "make disciples of all nations" (Matthew 28:19). When John described the countless sea of humanity gathered before the throne of the Lamb, he described them as coming "from every nation, tribe, people and language" (Revelation 7:9). To reflect the heart of God in expressing the issue-based passion for the lost, we must join Him in a relentless search for all nations.

## THE LAST-MILE PROBLEM

In the world of telecommunications, the last-mile problem refers to the challenge of delivering the final leg of connectivity from a communications provider to a customer. All the technology required to make the connection is in place, but "the last mile" of implementation is often disproportionately costly and challenging. More recently it has been used as a metaphor to describe the problem of bringing proven solutions to social problems to the final frontier of people who could benefit from them. For example, we know mosquito nets treated with pesticides will greatly reduce the infection and mortality rate, and at only $10 each, the cost is not a limiting factor. But the last-mile problem is cited as one of the reasons for the persistence of stupid death that keeps so many people dying from a disease that is so easily prevented.

Perhaps the body of Christ is suffering from the last-mile problem when it comes to making disciples of all nations. We know God has transferred the responsibility and authority of Jesus, the "true elder brother," to the church and commissioned us to embark on a relentless search for the lost from all nations (see Matthew 28:18-20). We have the resources needed to bring the good news to every corner of the earth, and yet there are still more than 2.5 billion people in over 6,500 people groups with little or no access to the gospel. Maybe we are facing a last *ten* miles problem. I have often wondered, *Has God stopped seeking, or have we stopped listening*? Since we know God is faithful and unchanging, the latter must be true.

---

We do an annual State of the Gospel update with Jason Mandryk, editor of *Operation World*. Use the one-time discount code chapter9#2-neighbor to download any of these annual webinar updates for free.

---

## MEASURING ACCESS

It is clear that not everyone has the same access to the gospel, but there are honest questions about how to quantify access. While there are many variables that could be considered, I simplify the conversation about access to the gospel by focusing on three important benchmarks: the strength of the church, the strength of the harvest force, and the scope of available resources, starting with the Bible. When considering these three variables, it is important to remember that we are focused on "nations" or people groups and not merely countries. Language is important, but even within the same language group there can be important social factors that create barriers as problematic as language (such as the differences and dislikes between Jews and Samaritans). India is one country but has as many as 415 languages and as many as 2,500 people groups! (For more information on people groups, visit www.joshuaproject.net.)

According to Finishing the Task (www.finishingthetask.com), as many as 639 people groups from seventy-seven different countries representing over half a billion people have almost no access to the gospel. Most of these people groups have no church and no believers. When it comes to the scope of available resources for evangelism and discipleship, nothing is more central than God's Word. According to the Last

Languages Campaign, there are 2,200 languages, touching nearly two hundred million people, who still need the Scriptures (www .lastlanguagescampaign.org).

It has been said that if you want to reach people no one else is reaching, you have to do things no one else is doing. I am a champion of innovation in missions and fully resonate with this statement. But I think we need to add, if you want to reach people no one else is reaching, you have to go where no one else is going. Paul the apostle said, "It has always been my ambition to preach the gospel where Christ was not known, so that I would not be building on someone else's foundation" (Romans 15:20).

The drive from my house in suburban Atlanta to my office is about twelve miles. In that twenty-five-minute commute I drive past ten of the approximately three hundred thousand Protestant churches in the United States. To put it in perspective, that is about one Protestant church for every one hundred people, compared to one McDonald's for every 2,400 people and one post office for every 940 people. I'm thrilled about the proliferation of churches in our country and agree with the premise that the best way to bring new people into the kingdom is to start new churches. There are no doubt hundreds, even thousands of lost people living in the same communities I drive through between my home and my office. But they are lost in plain sight. When considering the strength of the church, the strength of the harvest force, and the scope of available resources, they have more access to the gospel than perhaps anyone on the planet. Everyone has the same need for forgiveness, but not everyone has the same access to the gospel.

## IMPORTANCE VERSUS SEQUENCE

In the last few chapters I have been making a case that the highest PageRanked, issue-based passions of God are serving the poor, freeing the oppressed, and in this chapter, saving the lost. A common question you may be asking is "which of these three is most important?" Some would argue that these passions are inseparable in the heart of God and the question itself is flawed. Others would suggest saving the lost is much more important than meeting any temporal needs and look suspiciously on anyone engaged in compassion ministries that does not repeatedly offer a disclaimer about the priority of the eternal over the temporal, the soul over the body.

I think there is general consensus around the need for a both/and or "all of the above" approach that expresses the fullness of God's heart for the poor, oppressed, and lost. But agreeing on that point does not answer the haunting question, "What is the priority?" It is helpful to understand there is a difference between *priority* in terms of importance and *priority* in terms of sequence. With lostness, eternity is at stake. There is something much worse than any level of suffering or exploitation: hell. Forever. That makes lostness more important than poverty or oppression, though we must employ an "all of the above" strategy in order to reflect the fullness of God's heart.

But sharing the gospel, especially when serving people trapped by poverty and exploitation, is rarely a priority in terms of sequence. Upon arriving in a refugee camp where people are literally starving to death in hell-on-earth conditions, the highest priority in terms of sequence is giving them food, water, and other basic services. Although whatever practical ministry we provide is done "in Jesus' name," the initial priority in many contexts is given to serving rather than proclaiming as it relates to sequence. Even where the physical circumstances of the needy are not "life and death," when engaging people from a Hindu, Buddhist, or Muslim background, the process of communicating the gospel unfolds in layers of relationship, cultural sensitivity, and unconditional love, often at a pace that is much slower than what is appropriate for compassion ministries.

This distinction between importance and sequence is a point of confusion as well as caution. It brings confusion when those engaged in compassion ministries are wrongly criticized for giving priority, in terms of sequence, to physical needs. It is a point of caution when the emphasis on the horizontal (compassion ministries) indefinitely consumes the vertical (proclamation ministries). An "all of the above" approach that gives attention to poverty, oppression, and spiritual darkness as a reflection of the fullness of God's heart, does not suggest equal emphasis at every point in the journey. There is a difference between importance and sequence.

## OVERLAPPING CIRCLES: THE SWEET SPOT
## OF GOD'S COMPASSION

The overlap between poverty, oppression, and lostness is remarkable. It has been said that the lost are the poor and the poor are the lost. More than eight out of ten of the world's poorest people live in a geographic region of the world known as the 10/40 Window, a rectangular-shaped area from North Africa to the Pacific Rim, from 10 degrees to 40 degrees north latitude. An estimated 2.67 billion individuals living in approximately 5,710 unreached people groups are in the 10/40 Window. The 10/40 Window also contains the largest unreached people groups, over one million. In addition, the 10/40 Window contains the overwhelming majority of the world's least evangelized megacities—that is those with a population of more than one million. The top fifty least evangelized megacities are all in the 10/40 Window.[3]

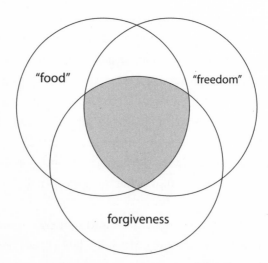

Everyone has the same need for "food," but not everyone has the same access to provision.

Everyone has the same need for "freedom," but not everyone has the same access to justice.

Everyone has the same need for forgiveness, but not everyone has the same access to the gospel.

God cares about every need, no matter who is involved or where that person lives. But as we have seen in these last few chapters, the Bible selectively emphasizes God's heart for the poor, the oppressed, and the lost. The overlap of these three circles could be seen as the sweet spot of God's compassion and a priority for our action. You can expect God to give you life-shaping experiences that heartlink you to these issue-based causes. As you refine your understanding of the highest purpose for your life, it will resonate with the PageRanked passions of God. Yet we must be careful to avoid extremes, recognizing that when Jesus clarified His mission by saying He "came to seek and save what was lost," He did it on the heels of personal ministry to a rich Jew named Zacchaeus (Luke 19:1-9). But it is also important to note that Zacchaeus, reflecting his sensitivity to God's prompting, immediately committed to reimburse those he had exploited as a tax collector, no doubt many of them poor, paying back four times the amount stolen. The overflow of Jesus' ministry to a rich Jew brought restorative blessing to others suffering under the weight of unjust power.

## AN UNLIKELY WITNESS

In 1997 I bought a yak. Purchasing long-haired, high-altitude livestock native to the Himalayan region doesn't sound like a very smart investment for a city slicker like me, so let me explain. In 1996 I led a group of church leaders on a prayer journey to Tibet. While there I had the opportunity to share with a small group of westerners in a Bible study and prayer group. During our prayer time I found myself in a small group of three consisting of me and two twenty-something young women from Europe; I'll call them Helene and Alexandra. I was struck by their passion for God and commitment to join Him in a relentless search for the lost in the region. At one point in our prayer time, I remember opening my eyes as they lay prostrate on the cold wooden floor, weeping and begging God to open a door for them to move to a very difficult region of Tibet to gain access to a specific people group. I was amazed at the fact that these two single women, smart, attractive, and filled with potential, were pursuing the highest purpose for their lives, one that connected their deepest sense of fulfillment with their greatest sense of accomplishment, in a very difficult place. I committed to pray for them and offered to do what I could to help them.

Now back to the yak farming. The next year I was contacted by these two girls who explained how a large region of China where Tibetan nomads live had been hit with a third year of severe winter, with the worst storms in fifty years. It had devastated the yak herds, killing by some estimates more than one million, as much as 40 percent of the yak population. Piles of dead animals could be seen by the roads. As many as eighty thousand Tibetan herdsmen had been affected. The Tibetan nomads rely on yaks not only for meat but for milk, clothing, shelter, and fuel. Herding families tend to be very poor, typically getting by on an income of between $100 and $300 a year. Money is earned by trading animals for grain or selling them or their meat for money. There were reports of Tibetan nomads, in total desperation, breaking into cars looking for food.

Tibetans in this region of China are among those with the least access to the gospel. They live with the frustration and unresolved tension of their ancient land having been absorbed by China. The combination of poverty and spiritual darkness was obvious. They were in the sweet spot of God's compassion, and it is no surprise that He moved on the heart of Helene and Alexandra to join Him in taking action. They hatched a plan to raise funds that would be used, under the direction of Tibetan nomadic clan leaders, to organize a livestock exchange whereby herdsmen who had yaks they could spare would sell them to the leaders, who would in turn give them to others who needed them most.

On a high grassland plateau, a meeting of Tibetan nomads was convened. It took several days for everyone to arrive. Helene and Alexandra had raised thousands of dollars to purchase yaks for a fair price and give them to nomads who were in desperate need. They wanted very much for this act of compassion to be done in Jesus' name and to open the hearts of lost people to how much God loves them, but it seemed impractical. This would have to be a time when lostness was a priority in terms of importance but not sequence. So they thought.

As the transaction was about to begin, their Tibetan friend, who was not a Christ follower, made some unexpected comments. He explained to the people gathered that Helene and Alexandra were not Tibetan Buddhists but rather followed Jesus. He reminded them that while influential and wealthy people from the West had sent money to their region, it went directly to monasteries and did very little to enrich their lives. But Helene and Alexandra wanted to make sure their actions were a blessing to the people, and they were motivated to serve the people because of their love for God. Amazing!

This is one example of what it looks like to take the initiative in crossing boundaries and overcoming barriers to show God's mercy by serving others. And though they were thousands of miles away from my home, our connected world provided the opportunity for me to become a yak farmer, partnering with two European women living in the sweet spot of God's compassion to bless Tibetan nomads I'll never meet, at least not on this side of eternity. Life in a connected world can seem like an out-of-control roller coaster, but what we are exploring together in this journey, the process of PageRanking your passions to fuel the highest purpose for your life in order to leverage your giftedness in ways that make an eternal difference, is not nearly as complicated as you might think.

Chapter 10

# WHAT IS YOUR LIFE?

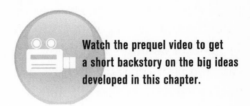

Watch the prequel video to get
a short backstory on the big ideas
developed in this chapter.

It has been said that if you can worry, you can meditate. It's the same skill set, just different thoughts. I would suggest that if you have ever been angry, you can be passionate. It's a similar mixture of primal emotions, just a different focus. That's important because I meet people on occasion who have struggled so long to discover their passions that it has become easier to believe they are destined for a passionless existence. They doubt if they will ever experience the combustible mixture of information, volition, and emotion associated with high levels of passion. You may be tempted to believe that the focus and freedom that come with PageRanked passion and a purposeful existence is for everyone but you. If so, I believe Amy Smith's[1] testimony has an important lesson for you; but before I tell you her story, I want to revisit some of the key ideas we've looked at so far.

## LIFE IN A CONNECTED WORLD

Life in a connected world is exhilarating and exasperating. We have more information than we could possibly manage along with faster, smaller techno-gadgets that have changed everyone's expectations about what it means to be accessible and informed. Physical proximity, as it relates to assigning responsibility for Good Samaritan activity, is important but incomplete. It is complicated by virtual proximity. And because in a connected world I'm virtually proximal to almost everyone on the planet,

I can learn about the needs of others, perhaps even see their faces, hear their voices, and know their names, in almost real time. Being one hyperlink away from tragic, chronic, and pandemic needs makes us increasingly vulnerable to information overload and compassion fatigue. The exit ramps between compassion and action are tempting. In this global village we're seeing more "wounded travelers" than ever on the side of the road. But it is easier than ever to justify passing by on the other side.

The goal of faithful Christ followers is not to filter out needs but to organize and prioritize them, to PageRank issue-based passions based on life-shaping experiences that heartlink us with God-ordained causes and intersect with His purpose for our lives. We are called to take the initiative in crossing boundaries and overcoming barriers to show God's mercy by serving others. Even if they aren't like us, don't like us, won't thank us, and can't repay us, which brings me back to Amy Smith's story.

## SERVE YOUR WAY TO THE TOP

Amy Smith is passionate about serving others. She has discovered that her hospitality gift along with her husband Carl's gift of giving and passion to develop people is a powerful combination that God will bless. But finding that sweet spot of service was a journey in itself.

After the birth of their first daughter, Amy found herself among the 10 to 15 percent of women who struggle with postpartum depression. The joy of motherhood existed simultaneously with loneliness and confusion, a desert season of the soul. Amy began to wonder, *Maybe we need a new church?* But that didn't help. Well-intentioned friends thought she may be harboring unconfessed sin; others suggested she should dig deeper in her personal devotions. In fact Amy was seeking God as desperately as ever. And though as imperfect as anyone, she was sure all her shortcomings were buried in the ocean of God's grace.

Then like the sun breaking through the clouds for a moment on a long, overcast day, Amy felt she heard God's answer: She was to serve her way out of the valley. That revelation led her to pray a powerful and dangerous prayer: "Let my heart be broken by the things that break the heart of God." Just as unexpectedly as the ray of sunshine that highlighted service, Amy sensed God prompting her with specific direction: Serve refugees.

Really? That was her husband Carl's response. Having grown up in Miami, he had a very narrow and stereotypical understanding of what refugee ministry might look like. But Carl was not only committed to serve alongside Amy, he was prepared to step up and lead the way. Within a week Carl and Amy found themselves reading a bulletin insert at their suburban Atlanta church, with a list of about sixteen ways to put your compassion into action. One of them jumped off the page as Carl scanned the options: Host a refugee family for a traditional Thanksgiving dinner. Hospitality and generosity were colliding with an opportunity to serve refugees. This had to be God.

Carl called the World Relief office in Atlanta to get more information, only to discover all the families had been placed. Maybe God was just testing to see if they were willing? On the contrary, He was simply making it easier for the World Relief office to deal with a last-minute cancelation. Carl got the call back, and the door was opened for a Liberian family to join the Smiths, along with another couple from their church, for a traditional Thanksgiving dinner.

Over turkey and stuffing, the Smiths would learn about the civil war in Liberia that killed as many as two hundred thousand people and produced one million refugees. About forty-five thousand refugees, including the family sitting around their dining room table, had made their way to a camp across the border in Ghana. Carl tried unsuccessfully to imagine what it would be like to flee your homeland, pushing your wife in a wheelbarrow because she had been hacked like tall grass in the bush by machete-wielding men in acts of cross-tribal violence. The Teamah family, now sitting comfortably at the Smiths' table, had spent the last fourteen years in a refugee camp, arriving in Atlanta just eight days before joining Carl and Amy for Thanksgiving dinner.

The sharing around the table exposed a common faith, and one of their new friends suggested they pray for Liberia and the people back in the camp. During the prayer time, Carl slipped away to encourage the children of both families to play more quietly. After the prayers came to a close, he offered a sincere apology for the background noise, saying a few minutes of peace and quiet was not too much to ask of the children.

Surprised by Carl's concern over the noise, one of their Liberian guests spoke up, saying, "Peace to us is no bullets." Those six words were chiseled on Carl's heart. They removed scales from his eyes and released a wellspring of empathy from deep inside his soul. Over the next few years compassionate action included driving lessons, job hunting, and ongoing discipleship, until two years later Carl had the privilege of accompanying Paul, a member of this family, back to the camp in Ghana to invest in church leaders with the goal of sending people back to the sixteen districts of Liberia for church-planting ministry. Paul was the first person to willfully return to the refugee camp after being resettled. He had started a church in the camp, and after receiving so much from his new friends in America, he just had to give back.

For Carl and Amy this Liberian family would become the first of a number of "wounded travelers" God would allow them to serve in His name. Amy marvels at how God can turn anything into an opportunity to bless others. The Smiths committed to host a Somali family of eleven arriving from a refugee camp in Kenya. Their existence had been so primitive that it was deemed they needed at least one week living with an American family before moving into their own apartment. They had never used an indoor toilet or even turned a modern doorknob. Carl and Amy were up for the challenge.

But in the middle of that hectic week, Carl's mother died; he had to return to Florida. This Muslim family watched with amazement and curiosity as Carl grieved, but not as one without hope. In a very natural and unforced conversation, Amy found herself sitting around the kitchen table explaining to her guests the reason for the hope that was within her and Carl. Death was being swallowed up by life as only God could do it.

It is a paradox of the kingdom that Amy, a "brokenhearted" woman struggling with depression, would find herself climbing out of the valley by asking God to break her heart even more, but for others. Our culture and our instincts would tell us to do whatever we can to keep our hearts from being broken. Her story reinforces the core message of the Good Samaritan, taking initiative to cross boundaries and overcome barriers to show God's mercy by serving others. How you respond to the needs of others depends on who you love the most. If you love God most, you will be others-focused, even when they are not like you and can't repay you.

## MANUFACTURING INTENSITY VERSUS CULTIVATING INTIMACY

Amy and Carl's story highlights the importance of surrender as a gateway to adventure. In response to God's counterintuitive leading to "serve your way out of the valley," Amy was willing to let God break her heart. When we surrender to God and yield to His leading, it opens the door to an adventure of obedience. Throughout this book I've been emphasizing the importance of identifying the passions to which you have been heartlinked by life-shaping experiences. These God-ordained passions fuel your purpose and greatly simplify the process of prioritizing your service of others, even in a connected world. But when life seems bland, as if someone has colored everything beige, the absence of true passion can spark a desire to manufacture energy in the form of intensity. Please don't succumb to that trap.

Intensity without passion is like a sugar high in the middle of the afternoon. It produces a burst of activity followed by more fatigue and less fulfillment. Intensity communicates, "I really want *you* to believe this." Passion communicates, "*I* really believe this." Intensity is marked primarily by emotion; passion is marked primarily by conviction. Intensity is perceived as superficial; passion is perceived as natural. Intensity is communicated by talking loudly; passion is communicated by talking plainly. Intensity drains; passion renews. Intensity can be an important supplement for passion but is never a valid substitute for it.

Manufacturing intensity is a temptation for everyone, but it is especially so with go-getters who want to make things happen. One of the most notable examples came in Howard Dean's 2004 political campaign. He had emerged as a front-runner in the buildup for the Democratic primaries. He was one of the first to successfully use the Internet to engage a younger demographic and mobilize the grass roots. But on January 19, 2004, Dean lost ground to John Kerry and John Edwards, finishing third in the Democratic caucuses in Iowa.

Dean wanted to encourage his beleaguered supporters amid his concession speech at the Val-Air Ballroom in West Des Moines, Iowa. He began the speech with clenched teeth, rolling up his sleeves as he spoke. When the crowd began to cheer, he raised his voice even louder, but the unidirectional microphone filtered out the crowd noise and left television viewers with a red-faced Dean shouting through clenched teeth, culminating with a list of all the states they were going to win beginning with New Hampshire, ending with the retaking of the White House. The speech concluded with a primordial and incomprehensible scream. Ironically, Dean delivered his concession speech on Martin Luther King Jr. Day; it was quickly and sarcastically dubbed "I Have a Scream" and posted all over the Internet.

Though Dean had enjoyed a 30 percent point lead in the polls in New Hampshire before the Iowa caucuses, he would come in second place there the following week, behind John Kerry, and one month after the red-faced rant in Iowa, his once promising campaign was over. In retrospect, I don't think anyone really doubts if Howard Dean was passionate about his campaign. But in that critical moment in Des Moines,  he tried to manufacture energy, and perception trumped reality. Manufactured intensity is not a substitute for authentic passion.

So what's the alternative?

If you haven't discovered and PageRanked your issue-based passions, you will be even more vulnerable to information overload and compassion fatigue in an increasingly connected world. But you can't manufacture passion, and you shouldn't try. Focus instead on cultivating intimacy with God, making surrender your daily priority. Embrace the adventure of obedience, affirming that you are more concerned about missing an opportunity to join with God in blessing others than looking foolish, being taken advantage of, or putting yourself at risk. Develop your giftedness, and look for opportunities to serve that will allow you to put your strengths to work. Give priority to the universal passions of the kingdom as reflected in the mission of Jesus. God is with the poor, the oppressed, and the lost; and He will be with you as you leverage your gifts to serve them in Jesus' name. Often the life-shaping experiences that heartlink us to issue-based passions come in the normal course of using our giftedness to serve others.

## THE POWER OF A CONNECTED WORLD

The curses of globalization can become the blessings of increased opportunity. In the hands of Spirit-empowered Good Samaritans, technological advances can set the stage for the "even greater things" Jesus said His followers would do (John 14:12). It has never been easier to grow your passion by learning, engaging, and influencing others. The power of a connected world opens the door for more information about your areas of God-ordained passion than any generation before us could possibly have imagined. It has never been easier to locate and network with others who share your passion. If you need passionate and gifted partners whose primary domain for engagement is discovery (solving a problem) or justice (righting a wrong) or advocacy (promoting a cause) or service (meeting a need), you are better positioned than ever to collaborate with them, even if your communication is entirely virtual.

It is no longer necessary to start a "brick and mortar" organization in order to mobilize others and make a difference for the causes you care deeply about. You may have already heard the amazing story of Zach Hunter. As a seventh grader he was studying about African American leaders during Black History Month. He was moved by the stories of abolitionists such as Harriett Tubman and Frederick Douglass, along with civil rights leaders such as Rosa Parks and Dr. Martin Luther King Jr. Zach wished he had been born earlier so he could have joined their struggle against the evils of slavery and racism. He was shocked to discover that there are more than twenty-seven million people trapped in slavery today. It wasn't too late after all to become an abolitionist.

As you might expect, Zach's passion fueled a self-directed interest to learn more about slavery, to engage in causes that make a difference, and to influence others to join him, even when sacrifice was required. As a teenager Zach launched a student-led fundraiser in his church and school called Loose Change to Loosen Chains (LC2LC). In its first year the campaign raised $8,500 for International Justice Mission's antislavery initiatives. He is leveraging the power of a connected world by making the LC2LC tool kit available as a free download from his website. As of this writing, it is available in English, Spanish, French, Portuguese, Korean, and German. Without a building or a formal organization, Zach is doing what passionate people do: influencing others to make a difference for the causes he cares deeply about.

## WHAT IS YOUR LIFE?

One of the most challenging passages in the book of James says, "Anyone, then, who knows the good he ought to do and doesn't do it, sins" (James 4:17). That verse reinforces a doctrine known as the sin of omission, as opposed to the sin of commission. A sin of commission is when we choose to do something we know God doesn't want us to do. A sin of omission is when we choose not to do something we know God wants us to do. Here's the entire passage:

> Now listen, you who say, "Today or tomorrow we will go to this or that city, spend a year there, carry on business and make money." Why, you do not even know what will happen tomorrow. What is your life? You are a mist that appears for a little while and then vanishes. Instead, you ought to say, "If it is the Lord's will, we will live and do this or that." As it is, you boast and brag. All such boasting is evil. Anyone, then, who knows the good he ought to do and doesn't do it, sins. (James 4:13-17)

Note the references to important life decisions such as where one chooses to live and for how long, as well as business priorities. In the middle of the passage, James asks a question, "What is your life?" which he answers with a powerful metaphor, "You are a mist that appears for a little while and then vanishes." I believe all of this builds momentum for how James wants us to apply verse 17, which highlights the sin of omission.

Here, as perhaps nowhere else in the Bible, we are warned against the dangers of making "life choices" that are not surrendered to God. It's a warning against taking exit ramps, an exhortation to follow your heartlinks in the brief days we have to do so. He is highlighting the sober and spiritual consequences of investing the passion and giftedness God gave you in self-serving ways that do not reflect the highest purpose for your life. This is not about missing one single Good Samaritan opportunity to show God's mercy by serving a "wounded traveler" on the side of the road. Nor is it a repudiation of business or profit. It is a specific warning to those who would waste an entire life, squander the sum total of all their "momentary decisions" in a whirlwind of self-absorption only to discover the mist of personal accomplishment is vanishing before their very eyes. "Anyone, then, who knows the good he ought to do and doesn't do it, sins" (James 4:17).

## RESPONSIBILITY VERSUS ACCOUNTABILITY

The question, "Who is my neighbor?" was asked to gain clarity on when God expects us to take responsibility for the needs of others. But there is another related and equally important issue we need to consider. God will hold us accountable for what we have been made responsible for. The level of accountability we have before God is related to two important factors. Jesus put it like this:

> That servant who knows his master's will and does not get ready or does not do what his master wants will be beaten with many blows. But the one who does not know and does things deserving punishment will be beaten with few blows. From everyone who has been given much, much will be demanded; and from the one who has been entrusted with much, much more will be asked. (Luke 12:47-48)

The two factors affecting the level of accountability we have before God are knowledge and resources. The more knowledge and resources one has, the higher the level of accountability. The stakes could not be higher for those of us privileged to live in a connected world at this moment in history. The world is getting flatter as we are in virtual proximity to needy people all over the globe. But it is also tilted. We have more information and resources that translate into even greater levels of accountability before God.

What is your life? How will you use it? I want to encourage you to embark on a passion-fueled journey toward the highest purpose for your life, one that glorifies God and takes initiative to cross boundaries and overcome barriers to show His mercy by serving others. I leave you with a few words of exhortation and encouragement from Zach Hunter:

> You don't have to look very far to know that our world is a messed up place. People are hurting. Suffering is everywhere. It can be really overwhelming. You might wonder why someone isn't doing something. Where is the help? Or you may think that if you're going to make a difference, it will be someday . . . when you're older, better educated, have more money, or have fewer problems of your own.
>
> Well, this morning when you woke up, there were people around the world and in your own community who were hoping that today might be the day. The day someone stepped in between slaves and their oppressors. The day relief from suffering begins. The day they could feed, clothe and educate their kids. The day someone showed kindness to them, or let them know they had value.
>
> Please. Know this—while you may not be able to do everything—and you can't solve all of the problems alone—working together, our generation CAN make a difference.
>
> Don't wait for someone else. Don't wait for someday. Because, YOU are the someone and TODAY is the day.[2]

Zach, I couldn't agree more. Anyone, then, who knows the good that could be done by crossing boundaries and overcoming barriers to show God's mercy by serving others, and DOES it, will find grace for that.

Go and do likewise.

# NOTES

## INTRODUCTION

1. Anya Kamenetz, "A is for App," *Fast Company*, April 1, 2010, 68.
2. Dan Ariely, a respected Duke University professor, has released a follow-up book to *Predictably Irrational*, called *The Upside of Irrationality* (New York: Harper, 2010). He is a recognized expert in the field of behavioral economics. In his new book he describes three psychological factors that affect how we respond to the needs of others as "closeness," "vividness," and "the drop in the bucket effect." Closeness is the same as proximity, though it can refer to relational rather than physical proximity. Vividness is similar to what I describe as urgency but is based on the amount of detailed and personal information available. The drop in the bucket effect is very similar to capacity, focused on how much impact will my action have? See chapter 9, "On Empathy and Emotion," Kindle location 3326–34.
3. Annie Zaidi, "Casteist Assault," *Frontline* 23, is. 2, January 28–February 10, 2006, http://www.flonnet.com/fl2302/stories/20060210003703300 .htm.

## CHAPTER 1: REDISCOVERING THE GOOD SAMARITAN

1. Reuters, "Jerusalem Monks Trade Blows in Unholy Row," Yahoo! News, July 29, 2002, http://dailynews.yahoo.com/.
2. I have modified a parable study outline introduced by J. Robert Clinton in his book *Having a Ministry That Lasts* (Altadena, CA: Barnabas, 1997).
3. Ted Dekker and Carl Medearis, *Tea with Hezbollah* (New York: Doubleday, 2010), Kindle location 4421–29, chapter 17.
4. Dekker and Medearis, Kindle location 245–53, chapter 1.

## CHAPTER 2: REDEFINING THE NEIGHBORHOOD

1. Ted Dekker and Carl Medearis, *Tea with Hezbollah* (New York: Doubleday, 2010), Kindle location 1436–45, chapter 5.
2. Michael Garofalo, "A Victim Treats His Mugger Right," March 28, 2008, http://www.npr.org/templates/story/story.php?storyId=89164759.
3. Garofalo.
4. Garofalo.

## CHAPTER 3: FROM INFORMATION TO ACTION

1. Norman Grubb, *C. T. Studd: Cricketeer and Pioneer* (Fort Washington, PA: Christian Literature Crusade, 1994), 119.
2. Grubb, 120.

## CHAPTER 4: TWO STREAMS OF PASSION

1. Frank Houghton, *Amy Carmichael* (Fort Washington, PA: Christian Literature Crusade, 1953), 115.
2. Sam Wellman, *Amy Carmichael, A Life Abandoned to God* (Uhrichsville, OH: Babour Publishing, 1998), 22.
3. "PageRank," Wikipedia, http://en.wikipedia.org/wiki/Pagerank.
4. "Corporate Information—Technology Overview," Google, http://www.google.com/corporate/tech.html.
5. Wellman, 23.
6. Wellman, 25.
7. C. T. Studd had served in both China and India before this final assignment from God in the heart of Africa.
8. In some cases *pascho*, Strong's reference number G3958, is translated as "suffered" or "suffering."

## CHAPTER 5: FOUR DOMAINS OF PASSIONATE ENGAGEMENT

1. Eric Metaxas, *Amazing Grace* (New York: Harper Collins, 2007), 92.
2. Metaxas, 91.
3. Metaxas, 91.
4. Metaxas, 94.
5. Metaxas, 107.
6. Metaxas, 110.
7. Metaxas, 132.
8. Metaxas, 110.

9. J. E. Hutton, "History of the Moravian Church," Christian Classics Ethereal Library, http://www.ccel.org/ccel/hutton/moravian.v.vi.html.
10. Hutton, http://www.ccel.org/ccel/hutton/moravian.v.vi.html.

## CHAPTER 6: PASSION-FUELED PURPOSE

1. Orison Swett Marden, *Rising in the World* (Cooper Union, NY: The Success Company, 1897), 111.
2. Eric Metaxas, *Amazing Grace* (New York: Harper Collins, 2007), 85.
3. Robert Frost, "Two Tramps in Mud Time," http://www.etymonline.com/poems/tramps.htm.

## CHAPTER 7: GOD'S PASSION FOR THE ULTRAPOOR

1. I found multiple sources in my research that use numbers ranging from 2,000 to 2,100. One of the most quoted is Jim Wallis, *God's Politics: Why the Right Gets It Wrong and the Left Doesn't Get It* (San Francisco: HarperSanFrancisco, 2005), 212–14.
2. Richard Stearns, *The Hole in Our Gospel* (Nashville: Thomas Nelson, 2009), Kindle location 751–56, chapter 4.
3. David Platt, *Radical: Taking Back Your Faith from the American Dream* (Colorado Springs, CO: Multnomah, 2010), Kindle location 1540–47, chapter 6.
4. "Genocide in Darfur, Sudan," Genocide Intervention Network, http://www.darfurscores.org/darfur. Getting reliable statistics on Darfur is difficult. Every group reporting has an agenda, some to downplay the tragedy and others to inflate it. No matter where you land, it is a tragedy that induces poverty by crisis.
5. Emily Wax, "A Loss of Hope Inside Darfur Refugee Camps," *Washington Post*, April 30, 2006, http://www.washingtonpost.com/wp-dyn/content/article/2006/04/29/AR2006042901223.html.
6. Stearns, Kindle location 1544–49, chapter 10.
7. Steve Monsma, *Healing for a Broken World* (Wheaton, IL: Crossway, 2008), Kindle location 1764–73, chapter 8.
8. P. Robinson, "St. Francis of Assisi," in *The Catholic Encyclopedia* (New York: Robert Appleton Company, 1909), http://www.newadvent.org/cathen/06221a.htm.
9. Lindsay Robertson, "Anderson Cooper: 'There's Just Stupid Death Happening Here Now,'" *Daily Intel*, January 16, 2010, http://nymag.com/daily/intel/2010/01/anderson_cooper_theres_just_st.html.
10. Stearns, Kindle location 1745–49, chapter 12.

11. Stearns, Kindle location 1777–82, chapter 12.
12. United Nations Children's Fund, *The State of the World's Children*, 2008.
13. Michael Finkel, "Stopping a Global Killer," *National Geographic*, July 2007.
14. *Global Issues Update*, August 2009, The Mission Exchange.
15. Stearns, Kindle location 1919–20, chapter 12.
16. Bono's comments were only a matter of weeks after the tsunami; the death toll would eventually surpass 200,000.
17. Bono, Keynote Address (National Prayer Breakfast, Washington, D.C., February 2, 2006), http://www.americanrhetoric.com/speeches/bononationalprayerbreakfast.htm.
18. Bono, foreword to *The End of Poverty: Economic Possibilities for Our Times*, by Jeffrey D. Sachs (New York: Penguin Books, 2005).

## CHAPTER 8: GOD'S PASSION FOR THE OPPRESSED

1. In diplomatic terms, this condition is referred to as "stateless."
2. International Justice Mission fact sheet—*Illegal Land Seizure*.
3. See Free the Slaves, http://www.freetheslaves.net.
4. U.S. Department of State, "Trafficking in Persons Report."
5. Kevin Bales in David Batsone, *Not for Sale* (San Francisco: HarperSanFrancisco, 2007), 1.
6. International Justice Mission fact sheet—*Bonded Slavery*.
7. From an interview on *60 Minutes*, CBS, March 21, 2010.
8. See UNHCR, The UN Refugee Agency, "UNHCR Annual Report Shows 42 Million People Uprooted Worldwide," http://www.unhcr.org/print/4a2fd52412d.html.
9. *Global Issues Update*, June 2009, The Mission Exchange with International Justice Mission fact sheet, Sex Trafficking and Commercial Sexual Exploitation.

## CHAPTER 9: GOD'S PASSION FOR THE LOST

1. Timothy Keller, *The Prodigal God* (New York: Dutton Publishing Penguin Group, 2008), Kindle location 714–23, chapter 5.
2. Keller, Kindle location 723–33, chapter 5.
3. See Joshua Project, http://www.joshuaproject.net.

## CHAPTER 10: WHAT IS YOUR LIFE?

1. The names in the story have been changed. The story is told with permission.
2. Zach Hunter, "Hey . . . ," http://www.zachhunter.me/#/hey-.

# ABOUT THE AUTHOR

STEVE MOORE has been engaged with Great Commission initiatives for nearly three decades. He has provided leadership for short-term teams serving in Europe, Asia, Africa, Latin America, and the Caribbean. He has traveled to more than forty countries working with church and mission leaders in a training and leadership development context. His life mission is to inspire and equip others—especially leaders—to live a focused life, finish well, and join with God in blessing the nations.

Steve is the president and CEO of The Mission Exchange (formerly EFMA), where he gives leadership to networking, training, coaching, and consulting initiatives designed to increase the effectiveness of the Great Commission community and accelerate the fulfillment of the Great Commission. He also founded Keep Growing, Inc., to train, resource, and coach leaders to leverage personal development for organizational effectiveness.

Steve is the author of *The Dream Cycle* and *While You Were Micro-Sleeping*. He holds an MA in intercultural studies from Fuller Theological Seminary. He and his wife, Sherry, are parents of four children and make their home outside of Atlanta, Georgia.

**Question:**
What do you get when you combine

**36** **book summaries**
*electronically delivered, 3 per month*

**24** **live webinars**
*average 2 per month*

**12** **author interviews**
*MP3 downloads, 1 per month*

**6** **global issues updates**
*bi-monthly downloadable webinar*

**3** **and 3 live conferences?**

See more details about the categories of membership and our member benefits on the following page.

New categories of membership include individual, church and educational affiliate beginning at $99 per year.

**1** **Answer:**
1 year of member benefits in The Mission Exchange

# Connect with The Mission Exchange

THE MISSION
**EXCHANGE**

*Empowering the Global Mission Community*

***TheMissionExchange.org***

# › Getting Connected

Getting connected with The Mission Exchange will open a door of shared learning, mutual accountability and trusted partnership with other like-minded evangelical mission leaders. We offer an innovative combination of online resources and live training events designed to add value to mission leaders and stimulate partnership.

To qualify as a **MEMBER** your organization must be a registered charity in the US or Canada, have at least $100,000 of annual revenue, agree with the National Association of Evangelicals statement of faith and be involved in cross cultural mission by sending missionaries or offering support service to the Great Commission community.

To qualify as an **ASSOCIATE MEMBER** your organization must be a member in good standing of another mission association that has been approved by The Mission Exchange board of directors. (Currently the only association so approved is CrossGlobal Link.)

We ask **AFFILIATES** to agree with the National Association of Evangelicals statement of faith as well as to affirm the vision, mission and core values of The Mission Exchange. There are three categories of Affiliate Membership:
· **Individual Affiliate**  - $99 per person
· **Church Affiliate**  - $279 for church wide staff, leadership and missionaries
· **Educational  Affiliate** - $379 for all professors, staff, students and allumni of a seminary, college, university or training program (such as DTS, etc.).

Note:  Affiliate memberships are available in our online store and are pro-rated based on the date purchased.

We encourage you to consider connecting with The Mission Exchange as outlined above but it is still possible to participate in training, networking events and live webinars as a non-member.  If you have any questions, feel free to contact us at Connect@TheMissionExchange.org.

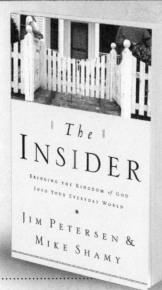
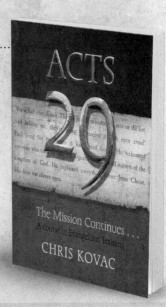